D1238808

HOW THE BIRMINGHAM CIVIL RIGHTS MOVEMENT CHANGED AMERICA AND THE WORLD

Barnett Wright
The Birmingham News

Edited by
Nicholas Patterson

Book design by Brooks Creative Media, LLC.

Library of Congress Control Number: 2012950487

ISBN 1-57571-050-1

This book is available individually or in quantity at special rates for your group or organization.
For further information, contact:
Carl Bates/cbates@al.com
Alabama Media Group
2201 Fourth Avenue North
Birmingham, Alabama 35203
205-325-2237

Front cover: The Rev. Fred Shuttlesworth (right) kneels in prayer during an April march in downtown Birmingham.
Back cover: From left: The Rev. Nelson Smith, the Rev. John T. Porter and the Rev. A.D. King on Palm Sunday lead demonstrators to City Hall.

Printed in Canada

Table of Contents

The Honorable William A. Bell Sr.

33rd Mayor

City of Birmingham, Alabama

Foreword

by The Honorable William A. Bell Sr.

On January 1, 2013, the City of Birmingham is opening its doors, inviting family and kindred spirits from around the globe to commemorate the 50th Anniversary of the 1963 Birmingham Civil Rights Movement for what we now recognize as the Movement That Changed the World.

But 50 years ago, the struggle that was televised across the world didn't look so noble. What seemed to many citizens as a disorderly commotion in the streets of downtown Birmingham in April and May of 1963 was in fact an organized protest. It was designed to force Birmingham to decide once and for all whether it would live up to the American creed "that all men are created equal."

The sit-ins, the boycotts, the pray-ins, the mass jailings, the mass street protests in 1963—all were coordinated under the leadership of the Rev. Fred L. Shuttlesworth of Birmingham's Alabama Christian Movement for Human Rights and Dr. Martin Luther King Jr. of the national Southern Christian Leadership Conference. They came prepared with the financial and legal backing of people from many ethnicities, organizations, and socioeconomic levels, including entertainers Harry Belafonte, Sidney Poitier, and Dick Gregory.

Together, these ministers led ordinary African-American men, women, and children in a nonviolent campaign against racial bigotry and social injustice.

By 1963, they could no longer wait for the permission of others to exercise their constitutional rights as any other American could. They had reached the limits of their patience that was tested daily with individual and collective slights and legal restraints that diminished their constitutional rights to "life, liberty, and the pursuit of happiness" that other Americans enjoyed.

Like other racially segregated cities in 1963, Birmingham had laws on its books like this one:

SECTION 369. SEPARATION OF RACES.

It shall be unlawful to conduct a restaurant or other place for the serving of food in the city, at which white and colored people are served in the same room. It shall be unlawful for a negro and a white person to play together or in company with each other in any game of cards or dice, dominoes or checkers. Every common carrier engaged in the operation of streetcars shall provide equal but separate accommodations for the white and colored races by providing separate cars...

Be It Ordained by the Commission of the City of Birmingham Failure to comply with this section shall be deemed a misdemeanor.

In a letter published April 12, 1963 in *The Birmingham News*, 62 black leaders pleaded with city officials to appoint a bi-racial committee to look objectively at the concerns that sparked the marches. "The current struggle in our community is an expression of the uttered or unexpressed deep yearnings of the heart of every

Negro in this community ... to say to our friends and neighbors of whatever race and creed, 'Let us live together in human dignity as American citizens.'" Their cries went largely unanswered. Even King's eloquent treatise on justice and humanity, "Letter from Birmingham Jail," also penned in April during his incarceration here during the Movement, was equally ignored. It wasn't until the Movement picked up new life as thousands of African-American children took to the streets in May 1963 that Birmingham's civic leaders were forced to rethink their position on segregation and consider Birmingham's image abroad.

The Rev. Shuttlesworth had already been leading the fight against segregation for seven years when he finally prevailed upon Dr. King to bring the Southern Christian Leadership Conference to Birmingham in 1963. Their combined goal was to create a situation so crisis-packed that Birmingham would have to come to an accord with its conscience.

Indeed, by 1963, some of Birmingham's white leaders had successfully orchestrated a campaign to oust Public Safety Commissioner Eugene "Bull" Connor from office. Their help in creating the new mayor-council form of government came from the relatively small number of blacks who were allowed to vote then. The new City Council that took power away from the likes of Bull Connor struck down all the city's segregation codes a few months after they took office.

Thus, by 1963, the majority of Birmingham was ready to move forward without the stigma of racial segregation clouding its future.

Yes, the transitions in 1963 were painful. The cost of our city's freedom was paid in the sacrifice of four little girls killed in the Sixteenth Street Baptist Church bombing, and two young boys who were also killed in September 1963. It was also paid with a stigma that still taints perceptions of our city.

But in 2013, the passing of time allows us to see Birmingham 1963 for what it truly was. Historical scholars have called the modern Civil Rights Movement "the Second American Revolution." And Birmingham 1963 was a key battleground in that revolution.

As the city embraces its unique place in world history 50 years later, Birmingham and its citizens as well as other Southern cities have organized more than 100 events to celebrate and remember the legacy of 1963, and the entire Civil Rights Movement, to humanity.

In 2013, the Mayor, City Council and citizens will designate the city of Birmingham as a Civil Rights Capital of Culture for a period of one calendar year. We are organizing a series of educational, cultural, and tourism events to celebrate the legacy of our collective civil rights heritage.

Birmingham 2013 is our opportunity to use its considerable cultural, social, and economic power to change the city's image and raise its visibility and profile on an international scale. We have the power to forge a new image of our city as open to progress and committed to civil and human rights for all.

We started building this profile in 1992 with the opening of the Birmingham Civil Rights Institute (BCRI), consistently one of Alabama's top attractions driving the state's $10 billion tourism industry.

Birmingham took history to the streets through its highly innovative Birmingham Civil Rights Heritage Trail. It features more than 200 interpretive signs with life-sized photographs of the Movement inserted into the streets where the 1963 campaign occurred, covering five districts citywide.

Part of the Trail includes a special City Hall display that includes ordinances like Section 369. It and similar laws are now relics of what will soon be an ancient past, put under glass with other records from the archives of the Records Management Department. Indeed, our city clerk discovered thousands of original documents that fully outline the ugly role that city government played from 1940 through the 1960s in denying citizens their rights based solely on the color of their skin.

These records add to the historical accounts of the blatant unfairness and the horrors of violence perpetrated against blacks and whites alike who dared challenge Birmingham's ironclad culture of racial segregation. But the records also show the bravery of lawyers, and the people they represented, who took the City of Birmingham to court, all the way up to the U.S. Supreme Court in many instances, and prevailed.

Many of the cases were the result of the unstoppable activism of one man committed to change: the Rev. Fred Shuttlesworth, the Bethel Baptist Church pastor who survived bombings and beatings in his struggle against second-class citizenship for African-Americans. It is said that he personally had more cases brought before the Supreme Court than any individual in American history.

So Birmingham, and all of America, owes its claimed birthright largely to our native son, the Rev. Shuttlesworth, who forced government officials in Birmingham and across America to live up to the principles of the U.S. Constitution that they were sworn to uphold.

Additionally, the City of Birmingham has invented the **Civil Rights/Sister Cities Program**, which is designed to stimulate cultural heritage tourism among Southern cities that played integral roles in the overall Civil Rights Movement. Those cities will include Montgomery and Selma in Alabama; Jackson, Mississippi; Columbia, South Carolina; Memphis, Tennessee; St. Augustine, Florida; Little Rock, Arkansas; Greensboro, North Carolina; and Washington, D.C.

In 2013 Birmingham will also host the National Conference on Civil Rights in September 2013, called "50 Scholars Speak on the 50th;" an international culture, food and book fair; a spectacular charitable gala; and Empowerment Sunday, which will include the 50th commemoration of the bombing of the Sixteenth Street Baptist Church.

Let us take time to remember the 1963 history, laid out in greater detail in this book. Let us refuse to let shame or anger deflect our reflections on anything less than the positive message that came from this history: that love always trumps hate, and that justice will prevail, and the roses of triumph can arise from the thorns of tragedy.

We invite all the readers of this book to Birmingham to help us share our history, discover our present, and share in shaping of the future, so that the city that changed the world can do so again.

Honorable William A. Bell Sr. was sworn in on Tuesday, January 26, 2010 as the 33rd Mayor of the City of Birmingham. He is a graduate of the University of Alabama at Birmingham where he received his master's degree in psychology and guidance counseling. He also holds a doctorate in jurisprudence from Miles Law School.

Lawrence J. Pijeaux Jr., Ed.D.

President and CEO

Birmingham Civil Rights Institute

Preface

by Lawrence J. Pijeaux Jr., Ed.D.

It's not very often that you measure the growth and progress of a city through one individual establishment or building; however, the Birmingham Civil Rights Institute (BCRI) lends itself well in this comparison. So much has happened in Birmingham, Alabama in the 50 years that have passed since the city's turbulent civil rights struggles of 1963 and I've only been in the city for the last 17 years. When Barnett Wright asked me to consider writing a preface for this publication, I had to really dig deep and think about my possible contribution—exactly what could I offer that others could not bring to the table?

After spending a few days thinking this over, I concluded that the best way to chart the city's growth since this pivotal time is to look at how it has embraced its history and how it has impacted civil and human rights issues around the world in a positive way. That history is all right here—at the Institute. In order to put it all into perspective, I must share a little history.

I remember riding the bus and sitting behind the sign that read "colored" in New Orleans, Louisiana in the early 1950s. On occasion, I would visit my grandmother who lived in uptown New Orleans. She was a very fair-skinned woman and would take me with her when she went shopping. Frequently, because of her skin color, we would ride the bus and ignore the sign and sit in front of it. I was too young to realize the implications that could have arisen from this action. It was a way of life that I accepted as a child.

My mother and I would often shop on Canal Street—the main commerce district during this period. Occasionally, we would stop at department stores and eat in our designated dining areas. Again, at the time it did not dawn on me that this was a discriminatory practice. But finally, the water fountains labeled "colored" and having to enter the movie theatre from a side stairwell that led to a balcony all began to add up. Even while attending church—I'm Catholic—I remember the large white church that my grandmother attended in uptown New Orleans. The two of us would always sit on one of the last two pews that were reserved for "colored" worshippers. This was a huge facility—however, we were relegated to those two back-row seats. Even when going to receive communion we were last—we had to take communion after everyone else. Can you imagine? Even the churches were segregated. The Rev. Fred L. Shuttlesworth, leader of the Birmingham Movement, was known for saying that "11 a.m. on Sunday in churches around the country is the most segregated hour in the world."

This was the life that I knew growing up in New Orleans. There was no place on earth that I could imagine was more segregated than this city. I had no idea that just over 300 miles away was a city that some referred to as "Bombingham." Once known as the largest, most segregated city in the nation, I did not know that one day the most significant experiences of my professional career would take place on its soil.

Former Birmingham Mayor David Vann visited a Holocaust museum in Israel and returned to Birmingham with a mounting interest in establishing a civil rights museum. Nothing could have prepared him for the opposition he would face. After Vann lost his bid for re-election and the city elected its first African-American mayor in 1979, his successor, Dr. Richard Arrington Jr., pledged that he would continue the commitment to build a museum dedicated to the individuals who gave their lives for equality. Arrington placed two different bond issues before the people of Birmingham that included revenue for schools, recreation and public works, and funding for a civil rights museum. Both times items involving the museum failed. Finally, through the issuance of general revenue bonds, Arrington was able to generate the $12 million necessary to build the museum. Once Birmingham's corporate community had the opportunity to view plans for the new facility, along with the storyline planned for the exhibition, they eventually came to understand the potential of this undertaking and offered their full backing, raising another $5 million to complete the exhibition and provide financial support through the first several years of operation.

After eight years of planning, the Birmingham Civil Rights Institute opened in November 1992. On that occasion, Founding President and Chair Emerita Odessa Woolfolk told *The New York Times*, "Some people say, 'Why open old wounds?' But I think it's wholesome. I think it's healthy." Nearly two and a half years later, when I arrived at the Institute in July 1995, I heard very similar comments. My usual response was, we will use the lessons learned from the non-violent Civil Rights Movement to create a brighter future. The mere idea of sharing Birmingham's civil rights history in a museum was not well received by the community at large. However, over the years, many of our visitors have shared comments echoing the sentiments of our founders, as well as the title of this book—*How The Birmingham Civil Rights Movement Changed America and the World.*

What have individuals said about our city and the significance of sharing the lessons of the Birmingham Movement with the world? During the 2002 collaborative conference *Transformative Justice: From Conflict to Resolution and Healing,* South African leaders Archbishop Desmond Tutu and former President F.W. deKlerk visited our city. On that occasion, Tutu shared in a luncheon speech that, "the courage of civil rights protesters who helped end segregation in Alabama inspired opponents who overthrew Apartheid in South Africa." And Beirut-based journalist Rami Khouri, a participant in the BCRI Oral History Project, has stated that "... The Birmingham Civil Rights Institute is a sign of the great strengths of American culture and Birmingham itself. One of the good things is that even when people are killed, they actually live on. The memory of those four girls who were bombed in the church is eternal, it's all over the world. And the man who stood in front of the tanks in Tiananmen Square in Beijing, in China. And the couple of kids in Palestine who were immortalized through news photography. Or Anne Frank in the Holocaust ... These are universal symbols of people all over the world, ordinary people, who do extraordinary things. And I think that's what the Civil Rights Movement was all about."

Other notable visitors include author and playwright Alice Walker and journalist Charlayne Hunter-Gault. After walking through the Institute, Walker reacted by stating, "... When you see this exhibit here at BCRI, it's just so easy to see how the struggle for civil rights, for human rights, is the struggle that connects us all over the planet." Hunter-Gault, the 2011 Fred L. Shuttlesworth Human Rights Award recipient, urged our community on by stating, "Even Arab Spring is reminiscent of the Civil Rights Movement. This was the beginning. One of the most powerful lessons of the Birmingham Movement is that of the power of nonviolence. Keep these stories so that they can inspire people who are committed to justice and free and open societies."

While it is encouraging to receive such comments from internationally-recognized visitors, it is equally heartening to hear from anonymous visitors to Birmingham and BCRI. For example:

Thank you for telling the story of a Movement that gave equality to all.

The whole country needs to come to this museum to know our history and how the historic struggles of people in cities like Birmingham defined and inspired freedom everywhere.

This experience really opened my eyes to civil rights and human rights here and throughout the world.

BCRI's renovation, completed in 2009, expanded the storyline chronicling Birmingham's progress beyond 1963 as well as highlighting the impact of the Birmingham Civil Rights Movement on other human rights initiatives worldwide. An example in our new Human Rights Gallery is a display showing the juxtaposition of former Birmingham Public Safety Commissioner Eugene "Bull" Connor's armored vehicle and a photo panel of military tanks in Tiananmen Square. In essence, the new Human Rights Gallery provides several examples that show how the Birmingham Civil Rights Movement has impacted other human rights movements. Additionally, we have an archives and research center that includes an extensive oral history collection. Over 400 individuals who were actively involved in the Movement—Black, White, Christian, Jew, rich and poor—have been interviewed. You can view segments of the interviews throughout the permanent exhibition as well as on our website and in the Richard Arrington, Jr. Resource Gallery at the Institute.

The Institute has hosted a series of teacher workshops over the years that were funded by the National Endowment for the Humanities. Titled *Stony the Road We Trod*, the workshops use the civil rights history from the Movement in Birmingham to help teachers learn how to teach the subject in their American history classrooms. The first workshop brought 200 teachers who participated—50 per week for four weeks. Teachers came from as far west as Hawaii and as far East as Boston. BCRI has several programs for middle and high school students. The Alabama State Department of Education funds the Birmingham Cultural Alliance Partnership (BCAP). Originally, the funding came from the Institute of Museum and Library Services (IMLS). Our staff works with Birmingham City Schools to offer this unique after school program that engages youngsters in hands-on enrichment at several of the city's most outstanding cultural institutions. Students learn about the contributions of African-Americans in those particular fields. The program has been well received and has earned national recognition. In 2006 and 2007, BCRI received awards at the White House for its work with young people in the Birmingham metro area.

The International Legacy Youth Leadership project is a partnership between BCRI and the Apartheid Museum and Mandela House Museum in South Africa. The project was funded by the Museums and Community Collaborations Abroad (MCCA) program, made possible by the U.S. Department of State's Bureau of Educational and Cultural Affairs and administered by the American Association of Museums (AAM). Between January and June 2011, project participants studied the roles of youth in bringing social and political change to the United States, through the Civil Rights Movement, and to South Africa as a result of the global anti-apartheid struggle. The project enabled youth in Birmingham and South Africa to then visit each other's countries.

Through special exhibitions and programs on a variety of topics, the Institute has connected with new audiences. *History Through Deaf Eyes* focused on the ***abilities*** of individuals who were deaf and hard of hearing. The exhibition gave visitors from throughout the community, as well as BCRI staff, a new vocabulary and appreciation for the ability to rise above life's challenges. *Triumph of the Human Spirit* and *Darkness Into Light* focused on the Holocaust and gave moving testimonies around the tradition of passing history from one generation to another. The *Living in Limbo* exhibition focused on lesbian families in Birmingham. It was our first attempt to address this subject matter in such a highly visible forum. The Latino New South project, led by the Levine Museum of the New South in partnership with the Atlanta History Center and the Birmingham Civil Rights Institute, is a unique regional collaboration designed to identify effective ways that museums can engage the growing Hispanic population in the Southeast in museum programs.

Since opening in 1992, the Institute has experienced tremendous growth in its educational reach locally, nationally and internationally as our city has grown during the same time span. Visible examples of our city's progress include the University of Alabama at Birmingham's prominence as an economic engine for the city and state, Railroad Park, Children's Hospital of Alabama, Regions Park (baseball stadium), renovation of the Birmingham Shuttlesworth International Airport and the Entertainment District and Westin Hotel. However, some of the issues from the past remain with us today. We continue to struggle with intolerance as evidenced by the new state immigration law, our failure to provide adequate public transportation and health care for the poor and elderly, as well as the alarming rate of black-on-black crime. There is a lot of work to be done and each and every one of us can be a positive force for change. Think about the Civil Rights Movement and how everyday people fought for basic equality. Their struggle was one that continues to have a positive impact on civil and human rights initiatives around the world.

On election night in 2008, I called my mother to discuss the results. My mother and I remarked that we never thought we would live to see the election of an African-American President. At that moment, I realized just how important the Birmingham Civil Rights Movement was in making that historic milestone a reality.

Lawrence J. Pijeaux Jr. is president and CEO of the Birmingham Civil Rights Institute (BCRI). Dr. Pijeaux began his tenure at BCRI in July 1995. A native of New Orleans, Louisiana, Pijeaux received his bachelor of science degree from Southern University in Baton Rouge, Louisiana; a master of arts in teaching degree from Tulane University in New Orleans, Louisiana; and a doctor of education degree from the University of Southern Mississippi in Hattiesburg.

Acknowledgements

I am indebted to a number of people who have been instrumental in helping me to write this book on Birmingham in 1963.

My mother, Dorothy R. Wright, gave my two brothers and me a set of great gifts when we were younger: the love of God and the love of books. Even though we grew up in a South Philadelphia housing project my mom took us to the library every Monday night to read and check out books.

While we could not afford to travel in person to locations around the world we were able to travel the globe in imagination. Books took us wherever we wanted to go and it never cost a penny.

So I must begin with gratitude and love for my mother, the greatest person I know.

Books allowed me to travel to New York and Paris, places I've always dreamed of. And, books allowed me to visit places I decided early on that I would never live such as Johannesburg and Birmingham, Alabama.

Never say never.

I moved to Birmingham in 2000 with my wife and two boys. My in-laws moved to Tuscaloosa and we came from Philadelphia to be near them.

The Birmingham that I found was nothing like the city of police dogs and fire hoses that I read about. I arrived with preconceived notions that proved false. The vast majority of people have been absolutely wonderful to me and my family. The city and area have problems like most places but I have nothing but good to say about visible growth and the maturity of Birmingham.

I never believed I would live in the city nor write a book about a key year in the city's history. I have done my best to present that history in the most thorough manner possible. That would not have been possible without the help of several people.

I have to thank employees of the entire *Birmingham News* company who were among the first to welcome my family when we moved to the Southeast. My colleagues made me feel at home and treated me as a member of their families. It would be difficult to name everyone, but I must acknowledge a few who were helpful personally and professionally.

Wayne Hester and Philip Pierce were my early editors and who were very patient. Editors Thomas Scarritt, Hunter George and Chuck Clark were also very instructive and supportive.

Pam Siddall, president of Advance Central Services of Alabama, came up with the idea for the book while president and publisher of Birmingham News Multimedia Company and remained committed to the 1963 project. Cindy Martin, president of Alabama Media Group, has also been a strong advocate of this project.

Staci Brown Brooks, Birmingham Community Hub Director and former director of Interactive Content for *The Birmingham News*, has provided support for the book. Vicki Applewhite, vice-president, strategy and marketing, Alabama Media Group, has been firmly behind these efforts. Thanks to Kevin Wendt, vice-president of content for Alabama Media Group, for his support and guidance throughout the process.

I would also like to thank The Honorable William A. Bell Sr. and his staff particularly Renee Kemp-Rotan for their help.

Carl Bates, director of business development for Birmingham News Multimedia Company, has worked from the outset to connect the project with the business community and brought along two key components: Nicholas Patterson whose edits have been invaluable and Teresa Brooks whose skills as a designer are unmatched.

I must also thank Dr. Lawrence Pijeaux Jr. and Laura Anderson Caldwell, at the Birmingham Civil Rights Institute; Voncille Williams, photo technician at the *The Birmingham News* and Amber Long, *The Birmingham News* librarian.

Thanks to Donald Wiley, formerly of *The Birmingham News*, for his patience and attention with the map of Birmingham, 1963. Thanks to my colleague and good friend William Thornton, of AL.com/*The Birmingham News*, for sharing his wisdom and historical documents.

Others who I have not met but are deeply grateful to are the historians, journalists and scholars whose books were instrumental in uncovering what happened in 1963. Their names are in the bibliography, but I want to single out Diane McWhorter and Taylor Branch for their magnificent writing and reporting.

Also, there would not be a visual record of 1963 without the men who captured the images, some who sustained injuries while doing so. They include: Robert Adams, Don Brown, Norman Dean, Anthony Falletta, Tom Hardin, Jack Hopper, Lou Isaacson, Ed Jones, Tom Lankford, Vernon Merritt, Charles Nesbitt, William Pike and Tom Self.

I can't end without mentioning a group of people and one particularly special person.

The people are the foot soldiers who have made Birmingham, the state, the country and the world a better place. I cannot imagine the courage that it took to go up against an entire police department and segregationists like Bull Connor. And many were mere children. But they did not back down. They wanted freedom and some put their lives on the line to achieve it. The four little girls murdered in the Sixteenth Street Baptist Church bombing did not die in vain. Their deaths prompted outrage that many now credit with passage of the 1964 Civil Rights Act.

The special person I want to thank is my wife Tanya. My wife has been the best copy editor, best friend, best mom and best counselor anyone could ask for. I can't put into words what she has meant to this project but, more importantly, what she means to me, Deion and Damon every day.

Barnett Wright is a government reporter for the Alabama Media Group. He and his wife Tanya have two children and live in Birmingham.

INTRODUCTION

The clock at the Sixteenth Street Baptist Church stopped at 10:22 a.m., the moment the bomb exploded.

Introduction

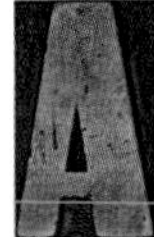

A phone rings inside the Sixteenth Street Baptist Church in downtown Birmingham, Alabama. Fifteen-year-old Carolyn Maull lifts up the receiver.

The date: September 15, 1963.

Maull answers and hears someone on the other end simply say, "Two minutes."

"They said that, and then 'click.' I was just standing there and kind of thought about it, hung the phone up, and stepped out into the sanctuary because I had three or four more classes that I needed to give these cards to," Maull recalls.[1]

A secretary at the Sixteenth Street Church, Maull is responsible for handing parishioners attendance cards and envelopes to record contributions. "Two minutes," she remembers the caller saying before hanging up. It is about 10:21 a.m. The temperature outside is forecast to reach a high of 75 degrees on the partly cloudy day.

Sunday school classes are just wrapping up. At the rear of the church in a basement corner lounge, a number of young girls are changing into their choir robes. Just a wall away, hidden beneath the back steps, are ten to fifteen sticks of dynamite. The dynamite explodes, blasting a gaping hole in the stone-and-brick east wall of the church restroom.

Maull recounts the dreadful event that followed: "As soon as I stepped out into the sanctuary—it wasn't two minutes, it was probably more like five seconds—something happened at that time. I didn't know the church had been bombed. What I heard at first sounded like a rumble, like thunder. I remember thinking rain—it immediately came to my mind. As soon as I thought rain, all of the windows started shattering, glass came pouring in.

"When that happened, I heard screams all upstairs, screams. Then somebody said, 'Get on the floor!' We all got on the floor and were very quiet for what seems like several minutes, but it was probably only twenty or thirty seconds. Then we heard footsteps at that point. Somebody had gotten up and started running."[2]

Following the detonation is a shower of bricks, stone, and steel that devastates the church lounge, shatters the sanctuary's stained-glass windows, and hurls large chunks of stone into automobiles and nearby buildings. It rips the clothes off the girls, killing four, decapitating one of them.[3]

When the blast goes off, Claude Wesley, 54, the principal at Lewis Elementary School, is having his car tank filled with gas at nearby station. His thoughts immediately turn to his 14-year-old daughter, Cynthia, who he had dropped off at Sixteenth Street Baptist minutes earlier. He abandons the car and runs toward the church unaware of what awaits.[4]

Firemen emerge with four battered bodies: besides Wesley's daughter Cynthia are Denise McNair, 11; Carole Robertson, 14; and Addie Mae Collins, 14.

Concerned parents either find their children at the church or hurry to hospitals to search there.

The Sixteenth Street Baptist Church bombing and the resulting deaths of those four innocent little girls rip apart the psyche of Birmingham, an already fragile municipality that some say is probably the most thoroughly segregated city in the United States at the time, with more unsolved bombings of Negro homes and churches than any other city in the nation.[5]

It is a city that five months earlier had given birth to a citizens' revolt, highlighted by children's marches that "subsequently struck the final blow to de jure racial segregation in Alabama and prompted the federal government to pass legislation prohibiting discrimination," notes educator and civil rights activist Odessa Woolfolk in *Black Workers' Struggle for Equality in Birmingham.*[6]

During those marches in early-April through May 1963, the Alabama Christian Movement for Human Rights (ACMHR) and the Southern Christian Leadership Council (SCLC) lead sit-in demonstrations at downtown-Birmingham lunch counters. Some department stores close their lunch counters altogether, while at others, demonstrators are arrested.

Throughout April and May of that turbulent year, thousands of demonstrators and marchers are arrested and jailed. Many are beaten and battered to the cement by water hoses. Some mauled by dogs. All of this brutality is endured in attempts to erase racial prejudice in a place some call "the Johannesburg of the South because of its history of racist domination," explains historian Horace Huntley in the preface to *Black Workers' Struggle for Equality in Birmingham.* "It also has been called Bombingham, the Tragic City, and the Magic City. In the 1950s and 1960s, black residents read the letters "MUN" on the licenses plates of municipal cars, particularly police cars as "Murder-U-Niggers."[7]

Huntley writes that the step toward betterment in Birmingham began gingerly in 1963 amid civil rights marches and church bombings. Those steps have moved slowly but progressively over the past 50 years.

Birmingham has risen from the remnants of those volatile times and now is home to the renowned Birmingham Civil Rights Institute (BCRI), which preserves the legacy of those who dedicated their lives to the cause of racial equality. Residents have embarked on a journey that has gone from "backwardness to betterment," Huntley says.

Since 1963, the city has gone from all-white political governance to a full inclusion of blacks in city leadership 50 years later and the BCRI is seen by many as a hallmark of the city.

"When visitors are brought to Birmingham, the Civil Rights Institute is very typically included on the short list of must see places," says Edward Shannon LaMonte, a retired professor of political science from Birmingham Southern College, in an interview. "That means 'must see' the ugly history, the pain of what the community went through and the gradual but consistent evolution in maturing that has taken place."

Change was felt beyond the city limits.

The 1963 citizens' marches and church bombings in Birmingham were harbingers of the Civil Rights Act of 1964, heralding a worldwide movement toward what many considered the promised land of racial justice. That landmark legislation, according to noted historian John Hope Franklin, is "the most far-reaching and comprehensive law in support of racial equality ever enacted by Congress."[8]

In 1963, all eyes were on Bombingham for

its racial intolerance. And now, in 2013, the city is proud to observe the 50th anniversary of the Civil Rights Movement and commemorate the struggle that served as a catalyst to transform Birmingham, the United States, and the world.

Numerous books have been written about civil rights in the 1960s, but few, if any, have focused solely on 1963 and the events that took place in Birmingham.

While 1963 is probably most remembered for the civil rights marches and church bombings, other events occurred during the year that helped shape the Birmingham of 2013.

In the spring of 1963, Birmingham elected a new set of officials to head a new form of mayor-council government; this proved chaotic when some argued the election that created the government was illegal and challenged the change to the Alabama Supreme Court.

In the fall, the city desegregated public schools for the first time, igniting a clash between Confederate-flag-waving protesters and police outside several schools.

All of these issues were covered in *The Birmingham News* and *Birmingham Post-Herald* but the role of the newspapers during the Civil Rights Movement cannot be ignored. Both failed to objectively cover racial events in their own city. "They missed the evolution of the Movement ... both papers made a decision to downplay the story," write Gene Roberts and Hank Klibanoff, in "The Race Beat: The Press, The Civil Rights Struggle and The Awakening of a Nation." While the local papers took what *Newsweek Magazine* called "an ostrich-like stance" regarding the events, major news organizations including *The New York Times*, CBS News, NBC News and The Associated Press provided dispatches that transformed a local story into national outrage at the way blacks were being treated in Birmingham by law enforcement.

The News was, however, doing its duty in reporting on other, more mundane matters in 1963. For instance, *The News* reported on the city's approval and encouragement of the state Public Service Commission's sale of its locally owned transit operation to a national outfit not long after Birmingham Transit Co. workers ended a 31-day strike. Also, city officials put up their share of money for the proposed Red Mountain Expressway, which would connect Birmingham with Homewood, Mountain Brook, and Vestavia Hills.

In many ways, life went about normally in many sectors of the city. In central Birmingham, construction continued on new building projects at the University of Alabama Medical Center, which steadily absorbed new blocks, according to newspaper reports. The facility was on its way to becoming the biggest single enterprise in Birmingham and the largest employer in the state. A few downtown structures were improved, too: one bank erected a new building, and a second financial institution increased in size. Still, front-foot after front-foot of other property in the downtown area was drab and decaying.

In the Birmingham of 1963, U.S. Choice round or sirloin cost 83 cents per pound, center-cut pork chops cost 59 cents per pound, and standard fresh oysters cost 89 cents a pint at the Liberty Super Market downtown at 420 13th St. North. A family-size 48-ounce bottle of Wesson Oil cost 59 cents, a dozen Miss Liberty grade A medium eggs cost 39 cents.

Everyday life in the city seemed much like that of any other American city in the early 1960s. But Birmingham in 1963 would leave its mark on history for a number of reasons. The year's events did not happen in a vacuum. The table had been set years before by the history of race-related violence in Birmingham and throughout the state of Alabama.

The conflict that erupted within the sleepy Southern city in 1963 thrust Birmingham into the national and international spotlight. And the events of that year started a political chain reaction that ultimately created the Civil Rights Act of 1964—the legislation that guaranteed for all Americans equal participation in public accommodations: schools, stores, restaurants, theaters, transportation facilities.

To fully understand the Birmingham of 1963, one must be familiar with the city's history leading up to that pivotal year.

Downtown Birmingham, 1963

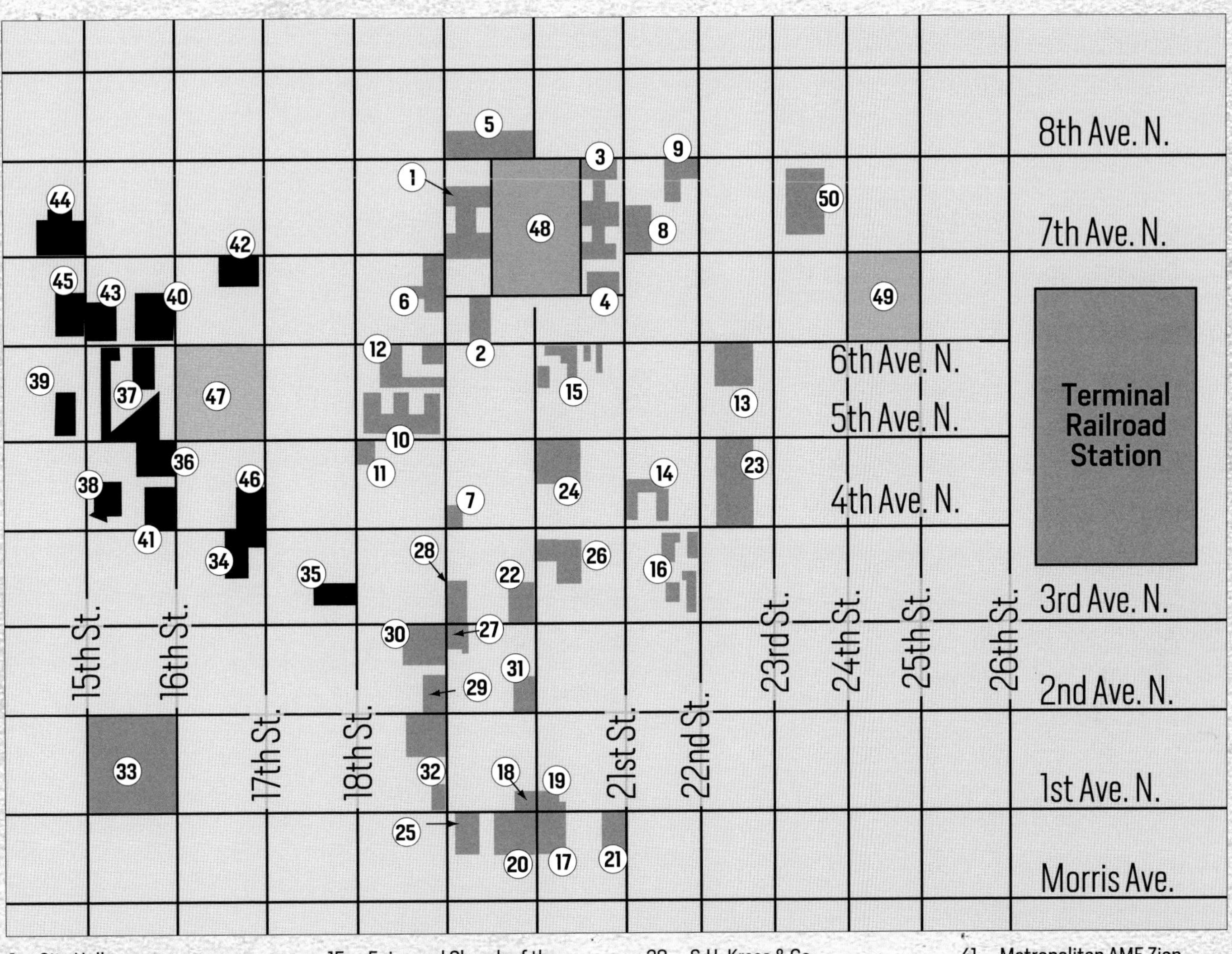

1 — City Hall
2 — Chamber of Commerce
3 — Jefferson County Courthouse
4 — Public Library for whites
5 — Municipal Auditorium
6 — Greyhound Bus Station
7 — Trailways Bus Station
8 — First Christian Church
9 — 2121 Building (FBI office)
10 — U.S. Post Office
11 — Federal Reserve Bank
12 — First Methodist Church
13 — First Baptist Church
14 — First Presbyterian Church
15 — Episcopal Church of the Advent
16 — St. Paul's Catholic Church
17 — First National Bank Building
18 — Empire Building
19 — Brown-Marx Building
20 — Woodward Building
21 — Protective Life Insurance
22 — Title Guarantee Building
23 — News/Post-Herald
24 — Tutwiler Hotel
25 — Britling Cafeteria No. 1
26 — Britling Cafeteria No. 2
27 — Woolworth's
28 — S.H. Kress & Co.
29 — J.J. Newberry's
30 — Loveman's
31 — Parisian
32 — Pizitz
33 — Sears, Roebuck and Co.
34 — Carver Theater
35 — Knights of Pythias
36 — A.G. Gaston Building
37 — A.G. Gaston Motel
38 — Gaston Funeral Home
39 — WENN Radio
40 — Sixteenth Street Baptist Church
41 — Metropolitan AME Zion Baptist Church
42 — Seventeenth Street AOH Church of God
43 — St. Paul's Methodist Church
44 — St. John's AME Church
45 — Sixth Avenue Zion Hill Baptist Church
46 — "Colored" Masonic Building
47 — Kelly Ingram Park (black)
48 — Woodrow Wilson Park
49 — Marconi Park (white)
50 — Phillips High School

■ BLACK INSTITUTIONS

Source: Glenn T. Eskew. But for Birmingham: The Local and National Movement in The Civil Rights Struggle. The University of North Carolina Press. Chapel Hill and London. 1997.

HISTORY
1871-1962

Birmingham, Alabama is incorporated in 1871 and located in the sparsely settled hill country of Jefferson County. The city begins with a population of 800.

History 1871–1962

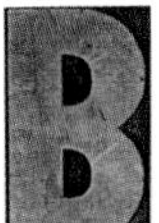irmingham, Alabama, was incorporated into Jefferson County on December 19, 1871, with an estimated population of 800.[1]

The new city was built on a parcel of land bought from the Elyton Land Company. It was located in the county's sparsely settled hill country, a locale avoided by enterprising farmers because the soil was unsuitable for the staple crops of corn and cotton. There had been a hint of the future in the area's crude industrial furnaces, which had been used during the Civil War to produce pig iron for the Confederate arsenal at Selma.[2] The furnaces were dilapidated, however, and Jefferson County offered no attraction to newcomers until two railroads were carved through it shortly after the Civil War ended. Where the railroads intersected, Birmingham was laid out.

Reconstruction laws gave the city an early boost by providing conditions favorable to a manipulated election that removed the new municipality from the neighboring village of Elyton and established it as the county seat. "Construction trains were brought into service on the morning of the election and hundreds of Negro laborers were hauled to town, as were large groups of white people," according to John R. Hornady in *The Book of Birmingham.*[3]

Local historians believe that black residents were duped into voting for the change of location by Col. James R. Powell, one of the town's most avid promoters, who also was president of the Elyton Land Co. and later elected Birmingham's first mayor. Mounted on a splendid horse, this impressive figure is said to have ridden among black people in the area, identifying himself as Gen. Ulysses S. Grant and urging them to vote for Birmingham as a personal favor to him.[4]

The city endured financial problems because of constitutionally imposed tax and debt limits that resulted in limited revenues from sales and property taxes. And fiscal challenges intensified sharply after the 1910 consolidation of Birmingham, which merged with three pre-existing farm towns, including, most notably, Elyton. The city grew from there, annexing many more of its surrounding smaller neighbors.

Birmingham in 1900 covered 11.4 square miles and had a population of 38,415. As a result of the consolidation, the city in 1910 had grown to an area of 48.3 square miles and a population of 132,685. It also had a large and growing deficit, and service demands that far outpaced the government's capacity to provide services. Each year the situation grew more dire.[5] According to all available sources, it is clear that the level of services and quality of life for black Birminghamians were significantly below the admittedly low standards of the community as a whole, writes Edward Shannon LaMonte in *Politics and Welfare in Birmingham, 1900–1975.*

Health care was virtually nonexistent. In

fact, among the city's black population, the death rate from tuberculosis of 349 deaths per 100,000 citizens was four times the white rate, LaMonte notes. In public education, the black-and-white comparisons were particularly stark. Early in 1873, the Elyton Land Co. donated land for the city's first public school. The deed specified how The Free School—its name, although a nominal fee of $1.50 was charged per year to reduce the debt associated with the school—was to be utilized:

> "To have and to hold to the Mayor and the Aldermen of Birmingham in trust as follows. For the use and purpose of erecting a schoolhouse and school buildings and improvements to be used under the management of the Mayor and Aldermen of Birmingham for the purpose of a free school for the white children now residing in and who may reside hereafter in said city and for no other purpose and use whatever. The school is to be taught by white teachers."[6]

The Free School, in North Birmingham, later became Powell Elementary School and closed in 2001. The 16,944 square foot building, Birmingham's oldest school building, on the southwest corner of 24th Street and 6th Ave. North, was still vacant when it caught fire in January 2011.

In 1905 Birmingham had eight elementary schools and one high school for white pupils; all

Birmingham in 1900 covers 11.4 square miles, but as a result of consolidation, 10 years later the city has a large and growing deficit, and service demands that far outpace the government's capacity.

were brick. The city had three elementary schools for black pupils: the Thomas School, which was the first brick building erected in Jefferson County for black students, and two frame structures, one of which was totally inadequate.[7]

Two years earlier, in 1903, *The Birmingham News* offered this assessment of the city's educational facilities for black children: "The east end Negro school is in miserable quarters. It has about 500 pupils who are packed into five rooms without light, without heating facilities, with distressing ventilation, and without desks."[8]

Black citizens petitioned the city's board of education for improved facilities in 1905, expressing concern about racial prejudice in the allocation of school funds. The board, however, felt the petition to be "ill-advised" and a "practical insult."[9]

Birmingham's black populace also was virtually excluded from active participation in Alabama politics. Locally, blacks had been barred from municipal politics in 1890 when the white Democratic primary had been instituted.[10] They continued to vote in state and national elections until the "disenfranchising constitution" of 1901—the same document currently used by lawmakers—which included "the most complicated and undemocratic suffrage article in the United States."[11] Of the 5,420 voters registered by officials during the spring of 1902, only 76 were black.[12]

Throughout the ensuing years, Birmingham's black citizens fared poorly when it came to municipal services. Part of the official attitude toward people of color can be explained by the virulence of the Ku Klux Klan (KKK) during the 1920s and its impact on local politics.[13] The KKK grew in Jefferson County after 1916, when the Robert E. Lee Klavern Number 1 was established; by 1924, this unit alone had an estimated membership of 10,000. The group's numbers peaked in 1926, when there were between 15,000 and 20,000 active Klansmen in the county, including two local judges, the sheriff, most members of the Birmingham police department, and at least 20 other city and county officials.[14] During the 1920s, aspiring politicians were compelled to honor, in word if not in deed, the KKK and its program of religious intolerance and racial bigotry.[15]

The Ku Klux Klan grows in Jefferson County after 1916 and its number peaks in 1926 with between 15,000 and 20,000 active members.

An incident during the Great Depression illustrates the prevailing attitude among public officials toward blacks in Birmingham. In January 1939, unemployed workers formed an integrated committee to press for more aggressive local efforts to secure Works Progress Administration (WPA) projects in the district. When a delegation of five whites and two blacks called upon the commission president, he shouted, "I don't care to discuss the matter with you. Don't come in here with a mixed committee. Don't bring Negroes in here on a committee."[16]

Tensions remained high between the races, and violence increased as blacks began to move into areas that previously had been all white. Bombings in 1947 during a zoning conflict between blacks and whites in the North Smithfield area established a pattern that spread across the South.[17] The North Smithfield community became known as "Dynamite Hill" for the number of bombs used to intimidate blacks moving into the neighborhood.

Associated Press reporter Ben Price wrote in 1952, "The dynamite stick apparently is replacing the burning cross and stinging lash in the South's pattern of violence." Between 1949 and 1952 bombers struck 10 times in Birmingham, as the black community struggled to expand into areas that historically had been populated by whites. After 1952, Birmingham Police records show that there were 28 bombings, bringing the total to almost 40 in post–World War II years, *The Birmingham News* reported.[18]

While 1954 was momentous nationally because the Supreme Court handed down its unanimous decision in the Brown v. Board of Education of Topeka, Kansas—stating that "separate educational facilities are inherently unequal" and making segregation in schools unconstitutional—Birmingham did not desegregate its schools until the fall of 1963. The city's opposition to the Supreme Court's decision was in lockstep with much of the rest of the South.[19] Only two Southern states began desegregation in 1954: Texas in one district, and Arkansas in two. Ten years after the Brown decision, only 1.17 percent of black school children in the 11 states of the former Confederacy attended school with white classmates.[20]

Other important race issues also were beginning to manifest in Birmingham around this time.

On May 26, 1956, the state of Alabama temporarily outlawed the National Association for the Advancement of Colored People (NAACP), which had championed rights and voting privileges since its founding in 1909. The Alabama Christian Movement for Human Rights (ACMHR) organized to fill this void.[21] Led by the Rev. Fred Lee Shuttlesworth's Bethel Baptist Church and 59 other black churches in the Birmingham area, the ACMHR's membership of preachers, deacons, Sunday school teachers, secretaries, and blue collar workers supported the organization with pennies or, at most, a dollar or two a week.[22]

For seven years prior to the widespread demonstrations that took place in Birmingham in the spring of 1963, despite numerous church bombings and constant threats and intimidation from the KKK and police, Shuttlesworth and the ACMHR created what some have termed the strongest Southern civil rights organization, and challenged every local segregation law.[23]

Many of the activities by segregationists alarmed members of the Birmingham Chamber of Commerce. First, they were increasingly dismayed by the inflammatory and inflexible actions of the pro-segregation city commission and especially Birmingham Commissioner of Public Safety Theophilus Eugene "Bull" Connor when it came to race relations. Particularly offensive to business leaders was the Mother's Day 1961 beating of Freedom Riders at the city's Trailways Bus Terminal.

The Freedom Riders, groups of blacks and whites seeking to integrate interstate transportation facilities, were savagely beaten when their buses came through Anniston, Montgomery, and Birmingham. Near Anniston, one bus was burned. While the riders faced opposition and violence during stops on their ride through the South, those incidents paled in comparison to what they encountered in downtown Birmingham, where they were met by a mob on what has been called "one of the bloodiest afternoons in [the city's] history." According to one historian of the period, police were absent from the station "because of previous arrangements with the Klan, which were made with the knowledge and approval of Bull Connor himself."[24] The attacks on the Freedom Riders shocked white moderates so much so that the Birmingham Chamber of Commerce began to consider a change of Birmingham's city government in 1962.

Most offended of all and destined to provide leadership for the reform effort, was Sidney Smyer, president of the Birmingham Realty Co.; a Dixiecrat in 1948 and a former supporter of the White Citizens' Council, he was the incoming president of the Birmingham Chamber of Commerce in 1961.[25] Smyer had been in Tokyo at the International Rotary Convention when a picture of the beatings appeared in the Japanese press. As a result, Smyer found himself the object of cold stares and perplexed questions from his Japanese hosts and the assembled international businessmen, who had suddenly lost interest in Birmingham's climate for investment.[26] Smyer became the first economic development representative of the city to have his efforts thwarted by the city's emerging negative international image.[27]

Partly because of the international embarrassment, the Birmingham chamber, with support from the Birmingham Bar Association, soon

A bus filled with Freedom Riders is burned near Anniston, Alabama. Freedom Riders, groups of blacks and whites seeking to integrate transportation facilities, receive savage beatings at some stops in the South, including the Trailways Bus Terminal in Birmingham.

pushed the change of government and recommended a strong mayor-council form of government. The Bar Association prepared a report recommending the new governmental setup and a group of young business professionals used their organization, the Young Men's Business Club, to adopt the report. Supporters of the mayor-council form of government got 11,000 registered voters to sign a petition backing the change and an election was set to abolish the city commission style of government.

Meanwhile, back in Birmingham, Shuttlesworth's ACMHR and Miles College students began boycotting downtown stores in early 1962. They sought the desegregation of facilities and the hiring of black sales clerks. While the boycott was effective, city businessmen said they could not overturn segregationist policies against the wishes of the pro-segregation city commission, one of whom was the outspoken Connor.

The Rev. Fred Shuttlesworth's Bethel Baptist Church is a frequent target of bombers. Here, he stands inside his church after the 1958 bombing.

In September 1962, Dr. Martin Luther King's Southern Christian Leadership Conference (SCLC) held its fall convention in Birmingham, and some white merchants painted over their segregation signs. But by October, after threats from Connor, downtown merchants had reestablished segregationist policies, and King said the SCLC would target Alabama, focusing on such areas as voter registration and integrating lunch counters.[28] Local black and white leaders asked that Birmingham be spared from any campaign until after a November change-of-government election, in which some hoped to end the influence of Connor. In November, voters approved replacing the commission setup with a mayor-council system; subsequent mayoral elections would be held in the spring.

Violence against the black community continued—with dynamite increasingly used as the tool of intimidation. Whites intent on thwarting any segregation efforts used the explosive to shatter black churches, dwellings, and business places.

On Sunday, December 16, 1962, after one of Dr. King's visits to Birmingham, a bomb exploded at Shuttlesworth's Bethel Baptist church. Twelve black children were practicing a Christian play in the church basement at the time of the explosion but none were injured, according to *The Birmingham News*.[29]

That blast would be a foreboding sign of what was to come in 1963.

JANUARY
TO MARCH
1963

George C. Wallace is sworn into office as governor and sets the official tone for the segregationist stance that will permeate the state as a whole and Birmingham in particular.

January to March 1963

The most memorable year in Birmingham history began with a clear, cold day. Temperatures were down to 25 degrees at 6 a.m. on New Year's Day, nothing out of the ordinary, according to city officials. During the 24 hours from New Year's Eve 1962 to New Year's Day 1963, ending at 7 a.m., the Birmingham Police Department received 249 calls and made 13 felony arrests and 44 misdemeanor arrests. Said a complaint clerk at City Hall: "Nothing unusual occurred. Just the routine drunks, fights, and scrapes."[1]

The city kicked off the year with at least one ambitious project: connecting to its surrounding communities. On Friday, January 11, contracts were signed to begin construction of the multimillion dollar Red Mountain Expressway. Beginning at the Birmingham city limits just northwest of Shades Valley High School and extending in the northerly direction to Woodcrest Road, the expressway was to run through heavily residential areas and business areas.[2] The estimated price tag for the entire project: some $12 million to $14 million.

The first phase of the project was worked out among Jefferson County officials; leaders from Birmingham, Homewood, Mountain Brook, and Vestavia Hills; and key figures in Gov. John Patterson's administration. This initial phase was scheduled to take 15 to 18 months to complete.[3]

The Birmingham Downtown Improvement Association and state highway officials said they were delighted with the proposed expressway because it would serve as a "relief" for the heavily traveled U.S. 31 that leads south from Birmingham to residential areas in Homewood, Mountain Brook, and Vestavia Hills.

Those relatively mundane matters for the first two weeks of 1963 paled in comparison to a powerful and portentous event that would have a profound effect on both the city and the state in mid-January.

On Monday, January 14, just 94 miles south of Birmingham, George C. Wallace took over as governor, and his inaugural speech set the tone for the segregationist stance that would permeate the state of Alabama as a whole and the city of Birmingham in particular. The oath of office was administered by Wallace's brother, Circuit Judge Jack Wallace. The newly elected governor spoke from the same flag-draped receiving stand in front of Montgomery's historic capitol building, where he stood for five hours waving amiably and nodding enthusiastically at thousands of marchers in the colorful inauguration procession.[4]

Early in his speech, Wallace exclaimed, "Today I have stood where once Jefferson Davis stood and took an oath to my people!

"It is very appropriate then that from this Cradle of the Confederacy, this very heart of

The Rev. Andrew Young and Dr. Martin Luther King Jr. met with other black leaders in early January to discuss the Birmingham Campaign. They are often the featured speakers at mass

the Great Anglo-Saxon Southland, that today we sound the drum for freedom as have our generations of forebears before us done, time and again down through history. Let us rise to the call of freedom-loving blood that is in us and send our answer to the tyranny that clanks its chains upon the South.

"In the name of the greatest people that have ever trod this earth, I draw the line in the dust and toss the gauntlet before the feet of tyranny ... and I say ... segregation now ... segregation tomorrow ... segregation forever!"[5]

Around the same time, black leaders throughout the South began to quietly strategize about how to combat the segregationist policies that oppressed black citizens in Birmingham.

In early January, a meeting was held in Georgia to discuss the Birmingham campaign. In attendance were Dr. Martin Luther King Jr., who headed the 365-day-long Montgomery Bus Boycott, which led to legislation that ended racial segregation on public buses in Alabama's state capitol; the Rev. Fred Shuttlesworth, pastor of Birmingham's Bethel Baptist Church and victim of several violent attacks in his struggle against racism in his hometown; the Rev. Ralph David Abernathy and the Rev. Joseph Lowery, Dr. King's right-hand men in Montgomery; the Rev. Wyatt Tee Walker, who followed Dr. King's Montgomery model to establish the Petersburg Improvement Association fight against segregation in Virginia; and the Rev. Andrew Young, who left a youth-outreach job with the National Council of Churches in New York City to lead voter-registration drives in Atlanta. All of these men also were key members in the Southern Christian Leadership Conference (SCLC), a group founded by Dr. King and dedicated to ending all forms of racial segregation. The topic of discussion at this gathering: Project C—for Confrontation.[6]

During the meeting, Walker revealed a blueprint for a campaign in four stages. First, they would launch small-scale sit-ins to draw attention to their desegregation platform, while building strength through nightly mass meetings. Second, they would organize a generalized boycott of Birmingham's downtown business section and from there, move to slightly larger demonstrations. Third, they would escalate to mass marches—to both enforce the boycott and fill the jails. Finally, if necessary, they would call on outsiders to descend on the city from across the country, as in the Freedom Rides, to cripple it under the combined pressure of publicity, economic boycott, and the burden of overflowing jails.[7]

Meanwhile, in a matter involving Birmingham politics, a petition was filed in Circuit Court and the Alabama Supreme Court on Thursday, February 14, seeking an injunction against the Birmingham Election Commission to halt the March 5 city elections. The petitioners, a pair of residents described as "private citizens" interested in "good government," did not want to see public money expended on an invalid election, according to an account in the *Birmingham Post-Herald*.[8]

Birmingham attorney S. Palmer Keith Jr., on behalf of the petitioners, argued on a number of fronts including the change-in-government election held the previous November was illegal. Birmingham voters had on November 6, 1962, elected to change the city form of government from a three-member commission to mayor-council. The February petition contended that the November election was "void" and of no effect because it was contrary to the public policy and

Mayor Art Hanes

March 1963 mayoral candidates, Tom King, Albert Boutwell, Eugene "Bull" Connor, J.T. Waggoner.

good morals in that it would have ended the tenure in office of persons duly elected to the office prior to the normal completion of their term. Keith also attacked the use of paper ballots in the March 5 election. If paper ballots were used, he argued, that would be contrary to two provisions of state law providing for the election, he said, according to an account in the *Birmingham Post-Herald.*

On Friday, February 15, the Alabama Supreme Court turned down Keith's petition for an injunction saying the lawyer had abandoned his rights to a hearing at the lower court level, according to the *Post-Herald.*

Five days later, the state high court denied a petition from Mayor Arthur J. Hanes to stop the election. Hanes had sought a temporary injunction to throw out the election. In a formal order the state high court ruled: "The granting or refusal of a temporary injunction is a matter of discretion, and election is a political matter with which courts of equity seldom interfere."[9]

The ruling paved the way for the Tuesday, March 5, mayoral race among former Alabama Lt. Gov. Albert Boutwell, Birmingham Commissioner of Public Safety Theophilus Eugene "Bull" Connor, attorney Tom King, and Birmingham City Commissioner J.T. Waggoner.

On March 5, in the midst of almost tornado-force winds and torrential rain, 44,736 voters went to the polls—at that time the largest number ever to participate in a local election. Boutwell received 39 percent of the votes (17,437), while Connor received 31 percent (13,788); 26 percent (11,639) went to King, and the remaining 4 percent (1,872) went to Waggoner.[10] Boutwell's margin was not enough to avert an April 2 run-off. Boutwell called for a change in leadership to bring a new era to Birmingham, which in 1963 was plagued with a lethargic economy and was a target of criticism because of its racial situation.

"I congratulate the voters of this city, on this day of storms and threatened tornadoes, the biggest number of voters who ever expressed their will in a city election went to the polls .... The vote which you have given me does not come as a surprise," Boutwell said after the polls closed. "Because I have felt from the very beginning, that the people of Birmingham were ready and eager for new leadership, for fresh ideas, and for a sense of abiding strength and unity in public affairs."[11]

Connor declared the upcoming April election a "showdown of whether two foreign-owned newspapers, one owned by Newhouse in New York and the other one by Scripps-Howard in Cleveland, (actually Cincinnati) Ohio, and the bloc vote are going to rule Birmingham or whether the people in Birmingham are going to rule themselves."[12]

In other matters in the city during the month:

Sunday, March 24: A heavy explosion resonated through much of Birmingham, destroying a black residence, injuring at least two people, and damaging houses and other buildings over a two-block radius. The blast tore a three-foot crater in the dirt alley in front of the house at 615 Second Ave. N. Five people were asleep in the house at the time of the explosion; two of them were taken to University Hospital.[13]

Sunday March 31: Birmingham Transit Co. operators and maintenance workers voted to go on strike, leaving almost 80,000 bus riders without their usual means of transportation. The Amalgamated Association of Street, Electric, Railway, and Motor Coach Employees of America, Division 725, voted 274 to 117 for the strike. Union leaders asked for a 45-cents-per-hour pay hike for all employees. A labor leader pointed out that operators were making $2.15 per hour and mechanics $2.33—less take-home pay than they were getting three years earlier, when a contract agreement was reached.[14]

APRIL
1963

From left: The Rev. Nelson H. Smith; the Rev. John T. Porter and the Rev. A.D. King march down Sixth Ave. North toward City Hall on Palm Sunday. They are stopped before reaching their designated location.

April 1963

Under warm, sunny skies, voters turned out in droves on Tuesday, April 2, for a historic election for Birmingham, which had been governed by a city commission for more than 50 years. On this day, a runoff would officially validate what the voters indicated they wanted in the previous November—a mayor-council form of government.

On the same day, April 2, Dr. King, Abernathy, and Walker got together at Birmingham's A.G. Gaston Motel, which would become a key meeting place for the growing Civil Rights Movement in Birmingham, to finalize plans for Project C—for Confrontation: huge, jail-filling, history-making demonstrations, during the Easter season.

In the election, Boutwell decisively defeated Connor in the race for mayor. Unofficial returns from the city's 151 boxes show that Boutwell took 29,630 votes to Connor's 21,648. Heavy voting all day pushed the total number of votes cast to 51,278—the highest turnout ever recorded in a local election, topping the former record of more than 44,000 in the March 5 primary. Connor, however, was allowed to retain his city commission office until April 15.[1]

Boutwell said he saw the election results "not as a personal victory, but as a victory of unity and harmony." He declared, "I see it as hope for every family whose breadwinner is out of a job. I look on it as an open invitation from the citizens of Birmingham to all our neighbors to merge their interests and boundaries with ours."[2]

Eugene "Bull" Connor

Connor wished Boutwell "the blessings of providence on the gentleman whom you have chosen as mayor when he enters upon the discharge of his duties, and I extend my heartiest congratulations." Nonetheless, Connor warned that the new era of government meant "government by remote control from newspaper offices, from the chamber of commerce, and from leaders of the minority group of 10,000 voters, none of whom are under oath as public servants."[3]

Boutwell's first act after being elected mayor was to send telegrams to the nine candidates named to the city council who would serve with him as leaders in Birmingham's changed formed of government—Dr. John E. Bryan, M.E. Wiggins, Don Hawkins, George Seibels, Alan T. Drennen Jr., Tom W. Woods, Dr. E.C. Overton, John Golden, and Nina Miglionico.[4]

The 1955 legislative act, under which Birmingham's form of government was changed and the mayor-council election was held, stipulated that the new officers should take over administration of the city on the second Monday following their election, which meant an April 15 inauguration for the mayor and city council.[5] But incumbent commissioners vowed a court fight and argued that they should be allowed to serve out their terms, which were to expire in 1965. Mayor-elect Boutwell and his council immediately filed suit to clarify the issue, but a final decision was not immediately forthcoming; the Alabama Supreme Court would not rule until May.[6]

Boutwell and the council were formally inaugurated on the steps of Birmingham City Hall on April 15. For the next six weeks, however, two bodies—each claiming that it alone had legitimacy—tried to govern the city. Between April 15 and May 24 Birmingham had too many governors but no recognized government.[7]

Mayor Boutwell moved into an empty office adjoining that of City Commission President and Mayor Arthur J. Hanes, and both men emphasized the absence of personal animosity. The mayor and council assured citizens that they would take

Mayor Albert Boutwell meets with members of the newly seated Birmingham City Council.

Police begin halting marchers before they can arrive at their destinations. Most of the demonstrators are arrested for engaging in protest activities, which have been banned by a judge.

no action that would compel municipal employees or the people to choose between two governments. The two bodies acted on identical agendas so that no question could arise about the validity of city ordinances or decisions; Hanes and Boutwell both signed all city checks.[8]

It was a city government crippled in its ability to act, unable to provide either leadership or a focal point for the resolution of community conflict. At precisely this time, the city faced intense open conflict in its area of greatest sensitivity: race relations.[9]

That was most obvious on Wednesday, April 3, one day after the city elections, when the Alabama Christian Movement for Human Rights (ACMHR) and the Southern Christian Leadership Council (SCLC) led sit-in demonstrations at downtown Birmingham lunch counters. Twenty-one participants were arrested at Britt's lunch counters. Kress, Loveman's, Pizitz, and Woolworth's closed their counters.[10]

The confrontations—the first strategy outlined by Walker in January during the planning of Project C—began during the first week of April. On Friday, April 5, ten sit-in demonstrators were arrested, including six in downtown Birmingham at Lane Drugstore (First Avenue and 20th Street) and four at Tutwiler Drugstore (Fifth Avenue and 20th Street).[11]

The next day, April 6, Shuttlesworth led a march toward City Hall, beginning at the Gaston Motel. Police halted the march at 18th Street and Fifth Avenue, arresting 32 participants.

On Palm Sunday, April 7, three Birmingham pastors organized protesters to march on City Hall. The Rev. Alfred Daniel (A.D.) King, younger

Above, blind jazz singer Al Hibbler is one of the first celebrities to show support for the Birmingham Campaign. He joins other protestors near the downtown Trailways bus depot. *Below,* arrests become the norm for protestors who are determined to end segregation.

brother of Dr. King and pastor of the First Baptist Church of Ensley; the Rev. Nelson H. Smith Jr., pastor of the New Pilgrim Baptist Church; and the Rev. John T. Porter, pastor of the Sixth Avenue Baptist Church, started their march at St. Paul Methodist Church (Sixth Avenue and 15th Street). On the way to their intended destination, however, marchers were stopped—26 people were arrested, and police dogs were used to disperse black onlookers.[12]

Among those arrested was then-20-year-old Elizabeth Fitts, who grew up in Titusville. She had attended Miles College and took part in the anti-segregation campaigns of 1962 and 1963.

> "In Birmingham during Easter week in 1963, I was arrested for demonstrating and placed in jail with older women who participated in the Movement. There were no mattresses on our cots, so we used our coats to make pads for the older women to sleep on. When the coats ran out, we asked the warden for Kotex pads to line the mattresses. I spent four days in that jail, and the food was horrible. The grits were brown, the eggs were powdered, and the biscuits were hard. I was very happy when I was allowed to go home. My mother was afraid for my safety, and she often stayed up until I came home."[13]

On Wednesday, April 10, sit-ins were attempted, but lunch counters were closed. Police arrested 27 protesters in the 400 block of 19th Street. Later that day Circuit Court Judge William Jenkins signed a court order banning black protests. Dr. King was the first person named in the injunction. To preserve public order and to prevent anticipated "bloodshed and violence," Jenkins specifically ordered 133 people not to engage in or encourage a host of protest activities: "parading, demonstrating, boycotting, trespassing, and picketing," even "conduct customarily known as 'kneel-ins' in churches."[14]

Dr. Martin Luther King Jr. writes his renowned "Letter from Birmingham Jail" in response to white clergy who believe the end of segregation should be pursued only in the courts.

Early the next day, Dr. King along with other leaders and many protesters who previously had been arrested received the injunction but decided to move ahead with the demonstrations.

On Good Friday, April 12, Dr. King, Abernathy, and Shuttlesworth led a march starting at St. Paul United Methodist Church in defiance of the injunction; they were arrested within yards of the site of the Palm Sunday arrests. During his incarceration, Dr. King wrote his renowned "Letter from Birmingham Jail."[15]

Written in response to a group of white clergy who were sympathetic to the cause but believed that the end of segregation should be pursued only in the courts, Dr. King's respectful response argued that civil disobedience was justified and necessary to end discrimination. The letter began:

"My Dear Fellow Clergymen: While confined here in the Birmingham city jail, I came across your recent statement calling my present activities 'unwise and untimely.' Seldom do I pause to answer criticisms of my work and ideas. If I sought to answer all criticisms that cross my desk, my secretaries would have little time for anything other than such correspondences in the course of the day, and I would have no time for constructive work. But since I feel that you are men of genuine good will and that your criticisms are sincerely set forth, I want to try to answer your statement in what I hope will be patient and reasonable terms."

Midway through his letter, Dr. King addressed the concerns of his fellow clergymen.

"First, I must confess that over the last few years I have been gravely disappointed with the white moderate. I have almost reached the regrettable conclusion that the Negro's great stumbling block is not the White Citizen's Counciler or the Ku Klux Klanner, but the white moderate who is more devoted to 'order' than to justice, who prefers a negative peace which is the absence of tension to a positive peace which is the presence of justice, who constantly says 'I agree with you in the goal you seek, but I can't agree with your methods of direct action,' who paternalistically believes that he can set the timetable for another man's freedom; who lives by the mythical concept of time and who constantly advises the Negro to wait for a 'more convenient season.' Shallow understanding from people of good will is more frustrating than absolute misunderstanding from people of ill will. Lukewarm acceptance is more bewildering that outright rejection."

Among the locals incarcerated at the same time as Dr. King was Jonathan McPherson, a Miles College faculty member who got involved in civil rights activism at the school.[16] One of the many Birminghamians who earned the title of "foot soldier"—everyday citizens who through their marching put their lives on the line for racial equality—McPherson recalls his arrest.

"When we participated in the Good Friday march in April 1963, we met at St. Paul United Methodist Church down below 16th Street. Andrew Young and Dorothy Cotton were there. They were keeping the audience inspired. We were just in anticipation. We wanted to put on our marching shoes. Dr. King was in conversation with the Kennedys—President [John Fitzgerald] Kennedy and Attorney General [Robert Francis] Kennedy—and they were trying to get him to call off the march. We had been there all that morning.

"About one o'clock, Dr. King came out and gave the word that we were going to march. We started and went up past Kelly Ingram Park and turned right at Fifth Avenue North and 18th Street. A white policeman wheeled his motorcycle in front of Dr. King and said, 'Halt, Halt!' We all fell down on our knees. They got the paddy wagon there and started loading us up. We went to jail. And that was my first time being in jail. But the unusual thing about it, when I got there, there was an elderly gentleman. His name was Mr. [William] Meadows. He was always at the Movement, and he was there in jail. I said, 'Brother

Meadows, what are you doing here? You are too old.'

"He said, 'I am going all the way. I want to see what the end will be like.'

"Now we were in jail. You could hear how the people would converse with each other. They wanted to see how Dr. King was doing. But they had a way that they were singing, and you could hear the singing coming from those cell blocks. We were in one part, and they had put Dr. King in isolation. That's when we later found that he wrote that 'Letter from the Birmingham Jail.' I stayed in jail overnight, and the next morning someone made bond for me."[17]

Carlton Reese, an organist at New Pilgrim Baptist Church who directed the ACMHR choir during in 1960s, was another foot soldier arrested during that period.18

"Many of us got beat on, but we kept going. We were instructed to keep going and not fight back because fighting back would only make the police retaliate. You had to know to get out of the way. There were many who got blasted by water hoses—knocked to the ground. But these experiences made us more determined to fight for our brothers. It was not just black folk; it was for white folk and other minority groups. The Movement was for anybody who needed to fight for their civil rights."[19]

Rather than serve blacks, most department stores choose to close their lunch counters.

On Easter Sunday, April 14, blacks protested in a way that some would have seen as radical, even during the height of the Movement: they attended worship services at predominantly white churches in the city, including the First Baptist Church and First Presbyterian Church. Several other houses of worship turned away other blacks who tried to enter. Approximately 1,000 people attempted to march to City Hall but were stopped by police; 32 were arrested including New Pilgrim pastor Smith and Sixth Avenue pastor Porter.[20]

Joe N. Dickson remembers that Easter Sunday well. Then an employee at A.G. Gaston's Booker T. Washington Insurance Co., Dickson was an organizer during the selective-buying campaign initiated by Miles College students against white-owned downtown stores in March 1962.[21]

"That was a time when I really understood what this Movement was about and what the real deal was," he said. "I was sitting right next

Police stop the Rev. Nelson Smith and the Rev. John Porter before they can reach City Hall.

to Rev. Porter, [who had been a pulpit assistant to Dr. King at Dexter Avenue Baptist Church in Montgomery]. They kept bringing folks into the jails. They had all the priests with their robes and things on. I said to Rev. Porter, 'We're losing this one. They're mad with Dr. King, saying he broke the injunction because he told us to march. They put him in jail. You're in here. Rev. Smith is in here. A.D. [King] is in here. We've lost this one.' You know what Porter told me? He said 'No, no. We are not losing this one, and we are not going to lose this one. Martin is working from on high. He's not working from down here.' "[22]

Johnnie McKinstry Summerville, a teacher and a regular at the mass meetings, described marching as "really rejuvenating."[23]

"I was doing something that would maybe help the race and myself. We learned to work together. This is what it took then. There were other teachers that I knew that were out there participating in the marches. We had to get out there and march and demonstrate. We really didn't think that we were going to get hurt or something was going to happen to us. We were out there trying to help. We were really putting ourselves on the line and we never thought about it. We never thought about being killed, being hurt, or being fired. We knew that it was necessary."[24]

Arrests were par for the course throughout April. On Thursday, April 18, demonstrators staged two sit-ins at lunch counters: one was closed, and demonstrators were ignored or not served at the other; no arrests were made. But that would change over the next few days.

Birmingham police arrest Parker High School student Mattie Howard in front of the Carver Theatre. Howard's arrest comes during the sixth day of the Children's Crusade.

On Friday, April 19, eleven protesters were arrested at the 2121 Building lunch counter. And on Saturday, April 20, seven picketers outside the Pizitz lunch counter were arrested, seven were arrested at a sit-in at Britt's, four were arrested inside Atlantic Mills, and seven were arrested inside at Tillman-Levenson.[25]

Annetta Streeter Gary was a member of the Peace Ponies, an all-girls club that became a vehicle for supporting the Movement. She remembered being jailed with the rest of her club.[26]

"I was arrested on Saturday morning, and I stayed until Monday night. It was an experience that just can't be explained. I remember the closing of the doors. We had one matron that came on in the evening shift who was not so bad as those other jailers. You could not eat the food, period. There was no way to eat the food. They had us scrubbing, gave us rags to scrub along the front of the cells. If you were too loud or whatever, you were given extra duties, extra things to do. At night, when the night matron came on—remember that I said she was nicer to us—she allowed us to bunk up with the ones that were in the back. So what she did was kind of double-up so that everybody could have somewhere to sleep."[27]

On Sunday, April 21, fifteen black worshippers attended white church services at the First Baptist Church, the First Presbyterian Church, and the Episcopal Church of the Advent. Blacks were turned away at First Methodist, First Christian, Woodlawn Baptist, Southside Baptist, and Highland Methodist churches.[28] Between Monday, April 22, and Wednesday, May 1, protests continued and sit-ins took place at Woolworth's, H.L. Green, and Britt's lunch counters. Demonstrators were not served, and no arrests were made. Protestors spent much of their energy in the courtrooms, fighting injunction and contempt-of-court charges. Mass meetings continued at various churches.[29]

At City Hall on Wednesday, April 17, the

Protests continue throughout the final weeks of the month as demonstrators demand human and civil rights.

Birmingham City Council members transferred all authority of the "former city commissioners" to themselves and declared any action by that body invalid without their concurrence. The three ousted commissioners—Hanes, Connor and Waggoner—contended that they were still the official government of the city, pending a court decision, and therefore ignored the incoming council's actions.[30]

On Tuesday, April 23, both the newly elected Boutwell and his city council and the outgoing city commissioners met to run city government. At the same time, presiding Court Judge J. Edgar Bowron ruled that the mayor and nine recently elected council members were the legal city government. In an order issued late that afternoon, Bowron held that Boutwell and the council members were "the duly elected" officials of the city entitled to legally assume the offices and duties of their respective positions.[31] Hanes, Connor, and Waggoner appealed the ruling to the Alabama Supreme Court.

In another matter:

Friday, April 26: Striking Birmingham Transit Co. bus drivers voted 201 to 162 to return to work. The settlement came as the transit company chairman revealed plans to sell the company to the American Transit Corp. of St. Louis. The union local approved a contract that called for an eight-cent increase for the first six months, a five-cent increase the second six months, five additional cents for the second year, five cents for the first six months of the third year, and two cents the last six months of the third year for all employees.[32]

MAY
1963

The Rev. Fred Shuttlesworth becomes a central figure in the demonstrations that will lead to concessions from Birmingham's white power structure.

May 1963

May would become one of the most important chapters in the Civil Rights Movement. The month began with Circuit Court Judge Jenkins on Wednesday, May 1, handing down sentences of five days in jail and $50 fines for 11 protest leaders held in contempt of court for ignoring his April 10 injunction.

But, the role of students from Birmingham elementary schools and nearby Miles College in the demonstrations during the month would lead to concessions from the city's white power structure and help loosen its grip over the black community. Those demonstrations were part of a Demonstration Day, D-Day—later named The Children's Crusade—strategy initiated by leaders of the SCLC.

Youths become an integral part of the Civil Rights Movement when the Children's Crusade begins on May 2.

Paddy wagons are often crammed with so many people that the doors will barely close, according to Movement participants.

The belief was that a mass infusion of students would be crucial to the success of any march in Birmingham. The students would be more cohesive and enthusiastic than some older adults.

The Rev. James Bevel, a 24-year-old preacher and a participant in several civil rights organizations, including the Student Non-Violent Coordinating Committee (SNCC) and the SCLC, had named Thursday, May 2, "D-Day" and Friday, May 3, "Double D-Day" in Birmingham.[1]

On Thursday, May 2, children, most school-aged, began the Movement's Children's Crusade, by demonstrating en masse against the Birmingham Police Department and Commissioner Bull Connor. Nearly 1,000 students gathered and moved east on Sixth Avenue and 17th and 18th streets. Ten of the groups converged on City Hall from all directions. Most of these young people were arrested in groups ranging in size from 30–60.[2] When the front doors opened to the Sixteenth Street Baptist Church shortly after 1 p.m., 50 teenagers—including James W. Stewart, a student at Ullman High School—emerged two abreast. The police officers stationed near the church gave notice of the court injunction against demonstrations, warned of arrest, and started loading the teens into paddy wagons.

"We were crammed into the paddy wagons that were meant to hold maybe eight people at the most, two in the four cubicles that they had," Stewart told Horace Huntley for the Birmingham Civil Rights Institute Oral History Project in 2003. "They crammed three or four of us into one cubicle, and they continued to press the door until they got it shut and locked. I was fifteen then."

While the paddy wagon was an experience Stewart said he was even more shocked by treatment in the jail.

"They put us in a holding facility that maybe should have held thirty people, and this was an empty room," Stewart told Huntley. "They put between three hundred and four hundred boys in the same room. There were so many people in that room that we had to sleep in shifts. Certain ones of us would lie down on the floor and try to sleep, and the rest of us stood around the walls or sat in the windowsills so that they could sleep. And when we couldn't stand any longer, we would kick them and arouse them and have them stand up, and then we would sleep. And this went on for the full four days I was in there. The toilet facilities were deplorable. At the end of this room there were five toilet seats, and that's how you went to the bathroom. You went to the bathroom in front of between three and four hundred people."

Stewart remembered that he was part of the first wave of students to leave the church on D-Day. Shortly after his group, a second double line of marchers came out of the church's front doors. They were followed by another and another. The police called in more paddy wagons and when that wasn't enough, asked the Jefferson County Sheriff to send in deputies. On running out of paddy wagons and sheriff's patrol cars, police called in school buses.[3]

On Friday, May 3, Bevel and one of Dr. King's top aides, Andrew Young, led even more students out of the Sixteenth Street Baptist Church, accompanied by the sounds of mass praying and singing and responsive chanting. More than an estimated 1,500 youngsters were absent from school that day. At 10 a.m., the students converged on Sixteenth Street Baptist and began filing out around 1 p.m. *The Birmingham News* reported that after two diversionary marches went west of the park, about 50 teenagers started marching toward the downtown area. Mayor Art Hanes, still acting in his role with the city commission despite an earlier court ruling that he no longer held the position, sporting a straw hat and standing at an intersection with Connor and a dozen cops, turned to Connor and said, "Here they come."[4]

Firemen earlier had reported that the water hose pressure was 50–100 pounds per inch. They turned the hoses on full blast and aimed directly at the youngsters, several of whom were skinned up as they skidded down the gutters under the intense water pressure.[5]

Carolyn Maull McKinstry, then a 15-year-old Parker High School student, vividly recalled the force of the water from the fire hoses.

> "The water hoses hurt a lot. I was hit with the water hose ... running from water. I had a navy blue sweater on. The water tore a big hole in my sweater and swiped part of my hair off on that side. I just remember the sting and the pain on my face. It was very painful, and you couldn't escape. There were a few points where we were trying to stand up and hold onto a wall. It was just a terrific pain from the force." [6]

Peace Ponies member Streeter Gary also recalled the incident.

> "We went down to Sixteenth Street Baptist Church. We went out in groups. As soon as one group cleared, then another group would go.[7]

Police and their German shepherds monitor activity outside churches.

One marcher recalls the force of water: 'I just remember the sting and the pain on my face. It was very painful, and you couldn't escape."

"The idea was that they were going not going to be able to handle all of us. They did not have enough police to stop us. Kelly Ingram Park, as far as you could see, was just people everywhere, which was a difference because, like I said, where we first started, the first couple of demonstrations that I took part in, there were fifteen to twenty people. This time, as we came out and we had our signs and all, I remember that I started crying when I looked up and saw all of the people. I guess it was just the idea of what was about to take place, the things that we had heard about, that Dr. King had talked about, how the Movement was moving forward. It was just overwhelming."[8]

The Double D-Day students were older, mostly teenagers, than the D-Day kids. A couple of the decoy columns walked right around a policeman who had ordered them to halt. The main group of young people was singing as they headed down Fifth Avenue North to 17th Street—to the threshold of what was considered "white Birmingham." On their right were more than 200 black adult spectators.[9] On their left, a crowd was gathering among the elms of Kelly Ingram Park. The marchers hesitated. The entire black district around Sixteenth Street Baptist was blockaded with police lines, squad cars, fire trucks. Fireman stood next to their rigs, sweating in their dun-colored slickers. "Do not cross," Connor intoned. "If you come any further, we will turn the fire hoses on you."[10]

Sixty young protestors were arrested in the first wave of demonstrations in or near Kelly Ingram Park. Several were attacked by police dogs. Bystanders threw bricks and rocks at the policemen and firemen. When the water drove them back they sneaked into buildings so they could lob their projectiles from above.[11] A white man was arrested when he attempted to drive his car into demonstrators. Twenty-seven demonstrators knelt and prayed at City Hall, where they were arrested and charged with loitering. Fifty demonstrators were arrested at 20th Street and Second Avenue.[12]

By Saturday, May 4, more than 3,000 protestors had been arrested since the start of the demonstrations in early April. Jails in Birmingham and throughout Jefferson County were filled to capacity, so many of those arrested were taken to the Alabama State Fairground, also known as Fair Park.[13]

Streeter Gary remembered some of what happened:

"My club members were there but we were separated. I think it was two, three, four of us together in one group, and three or four in another. We went around the corner, and I guess that must have been 17th Street; that was when the water hose met us. By me being small, I was one of the first ones in line along with one of my club members, Jackie.

"We had been taught that if they put the water hose on you, to sit down and cover your face so that the pressure of the water would not hurt your eyes. If we balled up into balls, then the water would not hurt as much. But that was not so. I can remember us balling up, hugging together, and the water just washing us down the street. Sitting and balled up, and the water just washed us down the street. Forceful. It was like pins maybe, sticking you in your arms and legs and things. The water was very, very forceful."[14]

Then-16-year-old Willie Casey walked out of Carver High School to join dozens of other students on their way to a mass meeting at Sixteenth Street Baptist Church. He offered this account: [15]

"When they started lining us up, I was about the twentieth person on the front row. We started walking for about two or three blocks singing 'We Shall Overcome.' Then the cops stopped us, let the dogs out, and put us in a paddy wagon. I was in the center of the paddy wagon. They crammed us in there like sardines. It must have been thirty of us in there. I don't know how long we sat there, but we sat there an hour or so in the heat of the day.

"Being young, it was no big deal to me. It was still fun at that point. They finally took us over to the city jail on Sixth Avenue and put us in cells. We must have been three hours or so in the cell. About three hours later, they came and got us and put us on a bus and carried us to Juvenile Court. It was dark then, must have been 8 or 9 p.m. It was cold, and all we had were light coats. We stayed in Juvenile Court for two or three hours. It must have been 1 or 2 a.m., and they put us on another bus. The Juvenile Court was full, so they didn't know where to put us."[16]

A parent, Nims R. Gay, who joined the Alabama ACHMR after the state government outlawed the NAACP in 1956, was part of the 1963 demonstrations. He remembered one of his children being slammed by water from the hoses.[17]

Birmingham Public Safety Commissioner Eugene "Bull" Connor, surrounded by media, points as marchers are arrested outside the federal courthouse on Fifth Avenue North.

"I witnessed my oldest son, Cardell, being washed down the street with a hose. This was one of the hardest things to accept. This is the time when you really have to control yourself. I would not have thought twice about hitting one of those firemen or policemen. I figured we could have won that battle with violence, but there is a hereafter, and you must stand before God to be judged. They were putting our children in jail and discriminating against us in every way. We knew the power of prayer, because if it had not been for prayer, a lot of us would not have made it."[18]

George Price was an NAACP member; ACMHR director of voter registration, committee member, and recording secretary; International Union of Mine, Mill and Smelter Workers Local 836 vice president; and USWA Local 6612 vice president. He, too, recalled the harrowing incidents.[19]

"During the demonstrations in April and May, we marched to the city jail on Sunday, and they would have the hose pipes and water. We prayed, and some of the preachers said they just wanted to go up to the jail to pray, and they refused to let us go. So some started walking off, and all of us walked off, and we went on to jail. But the fire department was out there with hose pipes to keep us from going to jail, just to pray. We had a lot of children, and vicious German shepherd police dogs, and the hose pipes were strong that they turned on any number of people. There were probably one thousand children. They knocked children down in the street and, at the same time, sicced the dogs on the people, and the children had to fight the dogs off. But they didn't have anything to fight the dogs with. The police did not do anything to keep the dogs off the people, nor did the fire department turn the water off."[20]

On Sunday, May 5, kneel-ins were held at 21 white churches. Also, a mass rally was held at the New Pilgrim Baptist Church (Sixth Avenue and 10th Street South); it culminated with a march to the Southside jail and a massive demonstration in Memorial Park across from the jail. This march was headed by the Rev. Charles Billups, of New Pilgrim, who led more than 1,000 people along the route before stopping at police barricades two blocks from the jail. At the barricades the group knelt and prayed. Firemen refused to use hoses on the demonstrators that day.[21]

On Monday, May 6, the demonstrations continued. Kelly Ingram Park was sealed off after many blacks had showered police with bottles and rocks during early marches. To reduce the chance of conflict with blacks who were not a part of the Movement, Connor had ordered his men to shut down the park, which had become a war zone.[22] The demonstrators kept marching. Comedian and activist Dick Gregory led 19 children out of Sixteenth Street Baptist Church for the day's marches. The police captain on duty called for the paddy wagon after the standard warning of arrest. The children came so continuously out of the church that police dispensed with the warning and led the demonstrators onto the paddy wagons and buses.[23]

Watching friends and relatives walk to jail at the rate of 10 per minute for nearly two hours, a number of protestors grew sullen and angry, perhaps compounded by guilt that they had not been willing to submit to the jailers themselves. A few bottles and rocks were hurled at police officers, landing on the pavement near them. Dr. King's aides, fearing that a riot soon would tarnish the largest single day of nonviolent arrests in American history, raced outside to call the demonstration to a halt at 2:40 p.m. By the day's end, nearly 800 people had marched to jail from church, and more than 200 reached the same destination from surprise picket lines in the downtown business district.[24]

On Tuesday, May 7, children continued to demonstrate—and Shuttlesworth was hospitalized with injuries inflicted by high-powered water hoses on the steps on the Sixteenth Street Baptist Church. Shortly before noon a group of 14 children marched out of the Sixteenth Street Baptist Church toward downtown.

Movement leaders made a strategic decision to flood the business district with masses of demonstrators. Many of the downtown businesses had been emptied of both blacks and whites. Business leaders began to realize the problems the city was beginning to face and the looming economic and social catastrophe, which former chamber of commerce president Smyer called a "black eye" for Birmingham.[25] The entire white business establishment was called by Smyer to an emergency meeting at the Chamber of Commerce to see what could be done.

Businessman Sidney Smyer

Meanwhile, at 10 a.m., Dr. King held another press conference at the Gaston Motel. Addressing the huge assembly of reporters, he said: "Ladies and gentleman, I would like to say briefly that the activities which have taken place in Birmingham over the last few days to my mind mark the nonviolent movement's coming of age. This is the first time in the history of our struggle that we have been able to fill the jails." Even as Dr. King spoke, young demonstrators made their way unobtrusively toward a dozen rendezvous points scattered around the business district.[26]

Meanwhile, at Sixteenth Street, Shuttlesworth was organizing groups of young protestors. While heading down the stairwell into the basement of the church, he heard a voice near the fire trucks on the street say, "Let's put some water on the reverend." Shuttlesworth looked up to see water arching toward him—100 pounds per square inch. He put his hands over his face and "spoke heart to heart with the Lord," saying, "If you're ready for me, I'll come." Then, a jet of water swept him down the stairs and slammed him against the wall.[27]

"Oh, my God, Rev. Shuttlesworth is struck," someone said. He was still trying to catch his breath when he was placed on a stretcher and loaded into an ambulance.[28]

Emma Smith Young, then 59, was a veteran of many demonstrations from Birmingham City

Hall to Selma. She was marching with her children when Shuttlesworth was injured. [29]

> "I was there at Sixteenth Street Baptist Church when Fred Shuttlesworth was hit with water and knocked off the steps of the church. My son, Dave, tried to go across and pick up Shuttlesworth, to keep them from killing him. Bull Connor was sitting across the street yelling, 'Put that water on the nigger.' He had them put the water on him, making Shuttlesworth go farther, farther, and farther down the sidewalk.[30]

Malcolm Hooks, 15 years old in 1963, grew up in Riley-Travellick, a black community in the southwest part of Birmingham. A student at Wenonah Elementary, he got involved with the Movement through his older brother and sister. Hooks provided a vivid description of the incident involving Shuttlesworth and the events that followed.[31]

> "When we arrived at the church, I was standing on the stairs waiting for the group I was assigned to line up with. As I waited, the police began using water hoses, and Rev. Shuttlesworth, who was next to me, was hit, but luckily my father pushed me out of the way. Rev. Shuttlesworth went over the railing and broke a couple of ribs and had to be hospitalized. Somehow, my father was able to see that danger was approaching, and he wanted to protect me.
>
> "Once Rev. Shuttlesworth was hit, my group quickly moved into position, and I remember my brother offered me a knife. I said no, because the Movement was strictly nonviolent, and I was obedient to the cause. My group continued to walk down Third Avenue North to the Holiday Inn, where we quietly took a seat in the lobby until a man from behind the desk said, 'Niggers can't sit here.'
>
> "Five minutes later, the paddy wagons came and escorted us to (the juvenile detention center on) Tuscaloosa Avenue Southwest. At midnight, my parents came to pick me up from jail, and I never saw a more beautiful sight than my parents waiting for me at the front.
>
> "Jail was a frightening experience, because some of the guys I was in jail with were older than me, and they were not in jail for participating in demonstrations. I was in eighth grade, and these guys appeared to be teenagers, but they looked rough. There was a lot of cussing and fighting among them, and when they asked if we participated in the demonstrations, they appeared to be curious.
>
> "They began telling us what they would do if they were in the same situation, and being nonviolent was not part of their approach. The overseer in the jail was a black man who called us niggers, and he was very intimidating toward us. It amazed me to see a black man have such opposition and hatred toward us because we were marching for freedom. I thought because we had a black man overseeing us that we would be more protected than if a white man were watching us.
>
> "Because he was black, we assumed he would be more sensitive to why we were there and realize that we were not there because we had done anything wrong. In fact, we were there because we were doing what was right.
>
> "When I first saw my parents, I was relieved because the supervisor had announced that no one would leave the jail that night because

Dr. Martin Luther King Jr., the Rev. Fred Shuttlesworth and the Rev. Fred Abernathy announce an agreement with members of the white business community and a suspension of the marches.

WSGN
610

of the lockdown at midnight. I was able to leave, and I was the last one able to go home. I thought I would have to spend the night, so I prepared a spot on the floor for myself, and I made a pillow out of my jacket. I knew that after the lights went out there would be a lot of fighting and arguing, so I was preparing myself for what might happen.

"I didn't believe that the nonviolent philosophy was going to protect me from the other juveniles I was in jail with. I wondered how I was going to practice nonviolence in jail when I was prepared to fight. I was obedient to the Movement cause, but I had to protect myself in the face of danger. Luckily, it didn't come to that."[32]

Protest organizer Dickson also remembered Shuttlesworth being slammed by the hoses.

"As I reflect on the struggle, I think about May 7, 1963, when we went uptown to get some kids out of J. J. Newberry and Co. Everybody was tearing up Newberry's and Kress'. They had gotten out of hand. Somebody called Sixteenth Street Baptist Church and said, 'Come get these children.'

"We went up to get them. Fred had a white flag. He led the children back toward Sixteenth Street. When he got to the Carver Theatre, the Birmingham Fire Department put a water hose on him and knocked him up against the theatre. He went down. He got up with a white flag. They put the water on him again. Some of the brothers who weren't participating said, 'Hey, don't put more water on him!' They didn't put any more water on him.

"He got on down to Sixteenth Street Baptist Church and got all the children inside the

Police use trained dogs to keep some older residents away from the march routes.

church. When he was going down the church stairs, the firemen put the water hose on him again and knocked him down. We thought they had killed him."[34]

By Wednesday, May 8, with behind-the-scenes mediation from federal officials, the demonstrations were postponed and Movement leaders said white business leaders were acting in good faith to settle issues of concern. Burke Marshall, Attorney General Robert Kennedy's assistant, had been in Birmingham to play a mediating role. Under his direction, black and white representatives met together for the first time in the office of Smyer, who had been embarrassed in Tokyo at the International Rotary Convention when a picture of the Freedom Riders being beaten in Birmingham appeared in the Japanese press.[35]

Negotiations to end the demonstrations lasted most of Thursday, May 9. On Friday, May 10, leaders of the demonstrations, represented by Dr. King, and the white business community, represented by Smyer, reached an agreement which included an end to the protests.

Dr. King said the agreement provided:

"1. Desegregation of lunch counters, restrooms, fitting rooms, and drinking fountains in downtown stores in planned stages within the next ninety days.

2. The upgrading and hiring of Negroes on a non-discriminatory basis, including the hiring of Negroes as clerks and salesmen within the next sixty days.

3. Arrangements for the release of all persons arrested during racial demonstrations on bond or personal recognizance.

4. Communications between Negroes and white persons to be re-established within the next two weeks."[36]

Walker announced a noon press conference at Sixteenth Street Baptist—but the church was crowded with marching shoes, just in case. Two o'clock came and went before Walker appeared in the motel courtyard with Shuttlesworth, Dr. King, and Abernathy.

They sat down, visibly tired, at a round metal table.[37] Shuttlesworth read a prepared statement:

"Birmingham reached an accord with its conscience today. The acceptance of responsibility by local white and Negro leadership offers an example of a free people uniting to meet and solve their problems. Birmingham may well offer for 20th-century America an example of progressive race relations, and for all mankind a dawn of a new day, a promise for all men, a day of opportunity and a new sense of freedom for America."[38]

As reporters fired questions about the sincerity of the white negotiators, Shuttlesworth said he wasn't feeling well and walked away to the applause of his crowd of supporters. But after taking a few steps he fainted.[39]

Bull Connor denounced the agreement and applauded the police and fire departments for "the wonderful job they have done to save segregation in Birmingham." He called the agreement the "lyingest, face-saving" statement ever issued. The newly elected Mayor Boutwell said the agreement was not binding on him and the city council. And former Mayor Hanes called the agreement "hogwash" and said he would order the arrest of any person violating the city's segregation codes.[40]

The city's governance had changed, but the new and old governments, at that moment, seemed to signal that the prevailing view of the white power structure remained resistant to the societal evolution mandated by the agreement.

On Saturday, May 11, the Gaston Motel and the home of the Rev. A.D. King were bombed. Three people were injured in the Gaston Motel explosion. King's family escaped injury.[41] Mrs. King said she was standing in the living room when the first blast occurred. The minister and his five children were in bedrooms in the rear of the house. The main blast tore a hole about four feet deep and five feet wide in the front yard, and the front of the home was heavily damaged. Outer walls were ripped apart and the interior was in shambles. [42]

At the Gaston Motel, a large hole was torn in the front of the building, the chief meeting place for Movement leaders. Another blast wrecked several houses next to the motel. Windows of stores in a two-block area were shattered by the force of the explosion. Motel rooms in the blast area were in disarray.[43]

The Rev. A.D. King's house is bombed one day after the agreement with the business community is announced. The front of the home is heavily damaged and the interior ripped to shambles.

On Sunday, May 12, reacting to the bombings and unrest in the city, President Kennedy sent U.S. troops trained in riot control to military bases near Birmingham and pledged that the federal government would "do whatever must be done" to preserve order in the strife-torn city. The president also ordered a proclamation and executive order to, if necessary, federalize the Alabama National Guard.[44]

The Army moved about 3,000 infantrymen, paratroopers, military policemen, and other troops to Ft. McClellan near Anniston and Maxwell Air Force Base in Montgomery, while officers of the Second Infantry Division from Ft. Benning and the Pentagon set up headquarters in the 2121 Building downtown.[45]

In related civil rights matters during May:

Monday, May 20: The Birmingham Board of Education issued an order directing the expulsion of 1,081 Negro students arrested in the demonstrations.

Wednesday, May 22: A federal judge ruled that the children were illegally expelled and ordered the student demonstrators to return to class.[46]

And in city-government-related business:

Thursday, May 23: The Alabama Supreme Court backed Birmingham voters in their decision to change to mayor-council form of government. The state high court ruled that Boutwell and the newly elected city council were the legal governing body of the city. The court rejected claims by the outgoing three-member commission that they should hold office until 1965.

The Supreme Court said it agreed with an earlier trial court that the mayor and councilmen be allowed to take their offices. The ruling read, "The trial court (the Circuit Court in Birmingham) held the mayor and councilmen be entitled to assume their respective offices, and the three city commissioners were prohibited from further use or usurpation or intrusion in purporting to act as commissioners of the City of Birmingham. Our conclusion is that the judgment of the trial court (Judge Bowron's decision for the mayor-council form) is due to be affirmed."[47]

Tuesday, May 28: U.S. District Judge Seybourn H. Lynne refused to order desegregation of Birmingham schools, setting up a legal showdown about schools in the city.[48]

JUNE
TO AUGUST
1963

Gov. George C. Wallace stands in the schoolhouse door to deny the entrance of two blacks into the University of Alabama. The students are later admitted.

June to August 1963

The civil rights demonstrations may have been postponed, but the reverberations from Birmingham rippled in other America cities and across the globe. The momentum from the protests would be overshadowed by Gov. Wallace's June 11 "stand in the schoolhouse door," an attempt to deny two blacks entrance into the University of Alabama.

But before that happened in Tuscaloosa, rallies of support for the protesters in Magic City came from as far as Birmingham, England, and Havana, Cuba. Clergymen in Greenwich, Connecticut, united to fight segregation, too. Elsewhere in the South, North Carolina's Duke University announced the admission of its first black students. Still, during a 10-week period after the settlement in Birmingham, statisticians counted 758 racial demonstrations and 14,733 arrests in 186 American cities. Protests had spread arrests to a locale almost every day in May: 34 in Raleigh, North Carolina; nearly 100 in Albany, Georgia; 400 in Greensboro, North Carolina; 1,000 in Durham, North Carolina.[1]

Blacks in other Alabama cities conducted demonstrations that were met with vehement opposition. In Gadsden, for instance, a city approximately 70 miles northeast of Birmingham, local police and helmeted state troopers joined forces in mid-June to disperse more than 300 blacks who were protesting the earlier arrests of their fellow citizens. The means of turning them away: nightsticks and electric cattle prods.[2] Also, in August, 300 blacks were arrested in Gadsden after battling with police officers, a few of whom wielded electric cattle prods to inflict pain on protestors who refused to get into cars.

Tuesday, June 11, began with two National Guard helicopters hovering over the University of Alabama campus. At 10:49 a.m. James Hood, of Gadsden, and Vivian Malone, of Mobile, arrived by automobile at the university's Foster Auditorium. They sat in the backseat of the second car in the convoy; two federal marshals were in the front.[3] Federal officials walked from their cars to the entrance of Foster Auditorium, where Wallace was standing, framed in the center of the door. Assistant U.S. Attorney Nicholas Katzenbach introduced members of his party and four times asked the governor to stand aside, telling Wallace:

> "I have with me a proclamation signed by the President of the United States within the last hour calling on you to cease obstructing justice. We came here to ask you now for unequivocal assurance that the students would get the education they should get."[4]

After Wallace refused the fourth request to stand aside, Katzenbach returned to the cars parked in front of the auditorium. The students were then led to their dormitories—Malone to

Mary Burke Hall, the girl's dormitory, and Hood to Palmer Hall.

At 11:45 a.m., Maj. Gen. Albert Harrison, head of the Alabama National Guard (ANG) received a telegram signed by Gen. Donald W. McGowan of the National Guard Bureau in Washington, D.C., federalizing the ANG's 500 members. The telegram informed Gen. Harrison that the "troops are now federal troops" and requested that Harrison call Washington "for further orders." [5]

At 3:33 p.m. — only after President Kennedy federalized the guardsmen to enforce enrollment—Wallace stepped aside to allow Hood and Malone to enroll at the University of Alabama. At 3:37 p.m., Hood walked down the sidewalk and into Foster Auditorium; he was accompanied by several Justice Department officials. Five minutes later, Malone, wearing a pink dress, arrived at the auditorium.[6]

Vivian Malone and James Hood become the first black students enrolled at the University of Alabama.

That night on national television, prompted partly by the events in Alabama, President Kennedy spoke of the discrimination and deprivation faced by black Americans. He said the nation was facing primarily "a moral issue ... as old as the Scriptures and ... as clear as the American Constitution."

Several other events over the summer in Birmingham showed that the city could be ready to move away from the hard-line segregationist stances of previous city leaders. [7]

On Wednesday, June 19, the city's Parks and Recreation Board voted to reopen at least three municipal golf courses: Roebuck, Highland, and Cooper Green by June 29. The decision brought to an end 17 months of closed courses. The shutdown had come following a November 1961 federal desegregation order and financial problems.

On Tuesday, July 16, more than 200 Birmingham citizens answered a challenge from Mayor Boutwell to help build a better city by serving as members of the new Community Affairs Committee. Membership included presidents of some of the area's largest industries, heads of civic clubs, housewives, ministers, educators. Participants threaded their way through an estimated 70 sign-bearing pickets at City Hall to enter the council chamber. The *Birmingham Post-Herald* reported that "man and woman, white and Negro, they paid little attention to the placards or those who waved them, as they gave their names at the door and accepted appointment to the committee simply by coming and being counted. They represent

A bomb planted under a tree at the right entrance of prominent lawyer Arthur Shores' Smithfield home causes damage but no injuries. Shores is one of the first blacks to practice law in Alabama.

every facet of the community."

And a week later the nine-member Birmingham City Council unanimously repealed all segregation ordinances in Birmingham as provided in the city's General Code. John M. Breckinridge, the city attorney, explained that the ordinances dealing with segregation of such places as eating facilities, ball parks, and auditoriums dated back more than 30 years and were unenforceable in the courts. The ordinances were compulsory, but, he said, had been declared unconstitutional in application by the U.S. Supreme Court, the appellate courts, and the U.S. District Court in Birmingham. Abolished were six ordinances involving segregation of restaurants, theaters, restrooms, entrances and exits, billiard halls, bowling alleys, and other such public facilities.

But, there were reminders that some were still not ready for change.

On Tuesday, August 20, a bomb exploded and damaged the home of prominent attorney Arthur D. Shores, one of the first blacks to practice law in Alabama; he handled countless desegregation cases. The charge detonated at 9:25 p.m. under a tree at the right entrance to Shores' two-car garage, but caused no injuries. Shores said he was at the opposite end of the house, lying in bed watching television, when an estimated six sticks of dynamite went off; his wife and daughter were at the movies at the time. Shores estimated damage to his home at about $8,000, with the heaviest impact in the two-car garage, where both cars

Attorney Arthur Shores

were parked, and in a recreation room above the garage.

In *The Gentle Giant of Dynamite Hill: The Untold Story of Arthur Shores and His Family's Fight for Civil Rights,* his daughter Barbara Sylvia Shores recalls that evening.

> "The crumpled roof of our home had collapsed and hung near the ground," she writes. "The garage doors had blown wide open, and inside I could see (my mother's) car crushed. The shattered glass from the house's windows lay all over the front lawn. The front side of our house had been demolished."

Shores also remembers the chaos in the neighborhood as angry residents took to the streets.

"The rioting terrified me," she writes. "Police struggled to get control of the mayhem. Broken bottles and glass covered the street and sidewalk. Men threw bricks at police cars, lashing out in uncontrolled anger. We tried to hold (my mother) up while we walked, but we could barely move through the mob of angry people. She was frozen with fear, and I heard her struggle to breathe. Somehow we held her up and pushed our way through the brawling crowds and flying bottles that barely missed our heads."

Shores also writes about the loss of her two dogs in the bombing. One, named Tasso, was killed. The other pet, named Rex, was never found.

> "Losing (Tasso) created a huge hole in my heart ...I still can't call his name or talk about him without crying. We never did find Rex, dead or alive. We think that when the bomb exploded, poor Rex just took off running and never came back.
>
> "I guess I can't blame him." [8]

Also in Birmingham:[9]

Tuesday, June 25: Directors of the Birmingham Improvement Association adopted a resolution urging the city council to utilize the Wallace Industrial Act, permitting the city to issue revenue bonds to attract new industry. Ironically, history would show that Alabama, and Birmingham in particular, lost significant economic development opportunities because of the protracted racial strife.

Sunday, June 30: Birmingham Police Chief Jamie Moore asked for a $540,000 increase in the police budget for fiscal year 1963–1964 and 94 more officers, emphasizing the heavy load placed on the department during the ongoing racial demonstrations. Moore argued that policemen faced massive civil rights protests from April 3 until May 9, unprecedented in his almost 27 years with the police department.

Friday, July 12: The Fifth U.S. Circuit Court of Appeals ordered Birmingham to begin desegregating public schools by fall. The court mandated that the city school board submit a desegregation plan to the U.S. District Court no later than August 19. The ruling overturned a May decision by U.S. District Judge Lynne, in which he refused to order desegregation.

Wednesday, July 31: The U.S. Justice Department filed suit against the Jefferson County Board of Registrars, following up on a threat to seek a federal court order requiring the board to instate more than 2,000 black voter applicants who had been rejected because they failed county qualification tests. The suit, filed in U.S. District Court in Birmingham, took no issue with the state's voter-qualification laws but accused the county of administering the laws to discriminate against blacks.

Monday, August 19: U.S. District Judge Clarence Allgood approved the Birmingham Board of Education's desegregation plan, as demanded by the Fifth Circuit Court of Appeals. The plan was for Birmingham to begin integrating in some 12th grades and possibly lower grades in all-white public schools. Under terms of the plan to put into effect the Alabama Pupil Placement Law without discrimination, all applicants for assignment or transfer for the 12th grade "filed in accordance with existing regulations of the Board of Education on or before August 26, 1963, will be duly considered."

Wednesday, August 21: Black attorneys asked for a federal court order requiring the Board of Education to begin desegregating all grade levels in the fall, instead of only the 12th grade as noted earlier in the month. The request came in a petition enumerating objections to the school board's plan for token desegregation of 12th grade classes and

U.S. District Judge Clarence Allgood approves the Birmingham Board of Education's desegregation plan as demanded by the Fifth Circuit Court of Appeals.

possibly a few elementary schools beginning on September 4.

Tuesday, August 27: Six buses departed from Sixteenth Street Baptist Church headed to Washington, D.C., for the March on Washington for Jobs and Freedom, scheduled for August 28. Organized by civil rights, labor, and religious groups and attended by blacks and whites, the march drew more than 250,000 to the nation's capital for what would become a historic event, where Dr. King delivered his still-enduring "I Have a Dream Speech."

Wednesday, August 28: During his speech from the steps of the Lincoln Memorial, Dr. King referred to the year's events in Alabama: "I have a dream that one day, down in Alabama, with its vicious racists, with its governor having his lips dripping with the words of interposition and nullification, one day, right there in Alabama, little black boys and little black girls will be able to join hands with little white boys and little white girls as sisters and brothers."

Friday, August 30: Birmingham School Board attorneys announced the three schools to be desegregated Wednesday, September 4: West End and Ramsay high schools and Graymont Elementary School. A total of five blacks were to be admitted at the schools, two each at West End and Graymont, and one at Ramsay.

Two years after his 'I Have a Dream Speech' in Washington, D.C. Dr. Martin Luther King Jr. participated in a historic Selma to Montgomery march for voting rights.

SEPTEMBER
1963

The explosion at the Sixteenth Street Baptist Church blows the face
[illegible]

September 1963

September was a pivotal month in Birmingham history for two primary reasons: the murder of four girls in the bombing of the Sixteenth Street Baptist Church and the turmoil surrounding the desegregation of three public schools over the vehement objections of Gov. Wallace and segregationists.

The bombing prompted international outrage that many now credit with bringing about passage of the 1964 Civil Rights Act. It remains, for many, the most horrific act committed by segregationists during the height of the Movement.

On Wednesday, September 4, police lines were established around West End and Ramsay high schools and Graymont Elementary School, the three white schools ordered to admit a total of five new black students. Hundreds of white demonstrators formed motorcades before school opening hours and went from school to school. At 7:20 a.m., members of the United Americans for Conservative Government gathered on the steps of Graymont with signs bearing slogans, such as "Close Mixed Schools" and "Keep Alabama White." Police asked them to move.[1]

A group of about 65 picketed West End High School first. Then they went to Graymont, where the crowd swelled to about 200, many of whom waved Confederate flags and anti-desegregation placards.[2] A handful of shouting white protestors set off street skirmishes with police after two black children registered.

Whites opposed to integrated schools gather early to object to the enrollment of two black children.

"Get the niggers out of that school," the group shouted. "Two, four, six, eight. We don't wanta integrate."[3]

The two black students were accompanied by their father along with Shuttlesworth and a black attorney. The school's principal said the students were registered without incident in his office in less than five minutes. School officials noted that many white parents kept their children away from school because they feared trouble.[4]

Above left: Josephine Powell, left, and Patricia Marcus, heading to class at West End High School.
Above right: Businessman A.G. Gaston: A bomb explodes outside his home.
Below: The Rev. Fred Shuttlesworth escorts two black students, their father and an attorney to the first day of school registration.

Outside the school, one group of about 25 protestors attempted to break through police barricades, and they were pushed back with nightsticks as more scuffles broke out. Some of the demonstrators called the police "Nigger lovers." [5]

It was estimated that more than half of the white parents refused to register their children. "Who wants to go to school," said one boy who had not been registered by his parents. "The niggers can have the place."[6]

That evening a bomb damaged the home of attorney Shores—for the second time in 15 days. Police said about two sticks of dynamite, possibly thrown from a car, blasted a crater two feet across and eighteen inches deep about six feet from the bedroom. Mrs. Shores, sleeping in an adjoining bedroom, was tossed out of bed and injured by flying glass. Shores and his teenage daughter were in another part of the house and escaped harm.[7]

In *The Gentle Giant of Dynamite Hill*, daughter Barbara Shores remembers what happened around 9:40 p.m.

> "Boom! Windows shattered hard on the floor around me, and the strong, pungent odor of dynamite shot up my nose, hurting like needles. Smoke enveloped the room, and I found I couldn't breathe. My knees buckled, and I fell to the kitchen floor.... I lowered my head and crawled. I felt my heart beating wildly, and I began to panic. I kept calling our father and mother as loudly as I could. Still no answer.... I could hardly see where I was going, but I kept crawling as fast as I could to the different rooms in search of them.
>
> "When I reached the front hallway, I saw daddy struggling to open the mangled front door. The bomb had blown the door partially inside the house, and it was stuck in the door frame, blocking the exit ... When I saw that daddy wasn't hurt, I stood up and ran to my mother's bedroom.... The explosion had knocked mother out of her bed, and she lay on the floor unconscious.... We later learned that she had slammed her head on the nightstand when the explosion threw her out of bed. The blast had also damaged the large glass chandelier above the bed, and a huge glass ball had fallen and hit her head ...daddy called our doctor, who came to our house and checked on mother. After about twenty minutes, she came to and opened her eyes" and the doctor said she would be okay, Shores writes.

For the second time in two weeks, a bomb causes damage but no major injuries at the home of attorney Arthur Shores.

Outside the house violent mobs of angry residents swelled. In a two-hour riot, 21 were injured and one killed, a 20-year-old black male who died at University Hospital after being shot in the neck. Blacks who lived near Shore's Center Street North home battled police after the bombing. *The Birmingham News* reported that blacks met police with bricks, bottles and rocks and cops shot the 20-year-old after he came from his house firing a gun. [8]

On September 5, the Birmingham Board of Education formally closed the three public schools following an informal decision reached after predawn telephone conferences with officials of the Wallace administration.

On Sunday, September 8, two firebombs were tossed at the suburban home of millionaire A.G. Gaston, one of the city's top black businessmen. Gaston, of course, owned the motel where the civil rights leaders met and where he often let them stay for free. He also provided financial assistance to the Movement. He owned the Booker T. Washington Insurance Company; Smith and Gaston Funeral Home; the Citizens Federal Savings and Loan Association and later founded the A.G. Gaston Construction Company. He also established the A.G. Gaston Boys & Girls Club which remains an integral part of the Birmingham community.

But Gaston was often at odds with leaders of the Movement. He opposed the children's marches and tried to talk Dr. King out of the Easter boycott of downtown businesses. Gaston preferred negotiating with the white business establishment over public confrontations.

One firebomb exploded inside the Gaston house, setting a lampshade, curtains, and rug aflame in the living room. The second bomb fell outside, scorching a wall of the house before fizzling out. No one was injured in the attack, which was the third recorded on a black home in less than three weeks. The firebomb, which officers said appeared to have been made of a gasoline-filled milk bottle wrapped in rags, did extensive smoke damage to the Gaston living room and throughout the house.[9]

Still, according to *The Birmingham News*, Gaston declined to fault the entire white community.

The bombing, he said, "certainly doesn't represent the majority of the citizens of the community. I believe it was representative of a very small minority of the community," he said.

On Monday, September 9, Wallace barred blacks from five state schools, which had been ordered to accept them. Alabama state troopers turned back blacks in Birmingham, Tuskegee, and Mobile.

On Tuesday, President Kennedy ordered the Alabama National Guard federalized and told Secretary of Defense Robert McNamara to use any of the nation's armed forces he deemed necessary to enforce school desegregation in Alabama. At Birmingham's West End High School, about 1,000 white students refused to enter the high school buildings after two black girls were enrolled.

As soon as the unrest arising from the school desegregation settled, another monumental event shook the city the nation, and the world—the Sixteenth Street Baptist Church Bombing.

The Sixteenth Street Baptist Church was the first black church to organize in Birmingham in 1873. Throughout its history, many prominent blacks in the city were members and many dignitaries spoke at the well-known place of worship. In the 1960s, Sixteenth Street served as a center of activity for the growing movement against racism in Birmingham and across the South.

Because of that, it became a target.

The explosion tears apart the basement wall at the Sixteenth Street Baptist Church, demolishes the women's lounge and leaves a gaping hole and a huge crater filled with debris.

The bodies of the four girls are found in the rubble. The force of the bomb knocks cars parked near the church backward four feet and dents the vehicles with large holes caused by flying debris. Nearby buildings are in shambles and some are windowless.

At the time of the church explosion on Sunday, September 15, about 200 parishioners were in the building, recalled Sunday school teacher Effie J. McCaw, who was in the church at the time of the blast. Debris came crashing down in the rear of the church, she recalled, and several people were cut and bruised. Giant stained-glass windows—18 feet wide by 23 feet tall—were shattered. One of the windows depicted Jesus Christ leading a group of children. After the blast, Christ's head was blown away; his body remained. A skylight fell directly on the pulpit. Stairs leading from the sanctuary to the basement were splintered. The banister, turned loose, looked like a picket fence.

A huge crater was dug by the blast at the 16th Street entrance. The concrete steps that led to the main-floor sanctuary from the side door were blown away. A police detective said the bomb had been placed in a rarely used stairwell outside the restroom. Members of the Ku Klux Klan were immediately suspected in the bombing.[10]

Inside, the rear section of church was in shambles. The force of the blast twisted chairs, shredded wooden benches, and knocked out windows. Even a block away, windows were blown out of buildings, and occupants of houses said they were jolted off their feet. Police at City Hall, three blocks away, at the time said the building seemed to shudder.

McCaw recalled the devastating incident:

> "We were all in Sunday school classrooms when the bomb went off. I told the children in my class to lie on the floor. The teachers kept the congregation from panicking. We couldn't get to the children in the basement. Everyone walked outside in a hurry. There was no screaming, only crying."[11]

Denise McNair

Carole Robertson

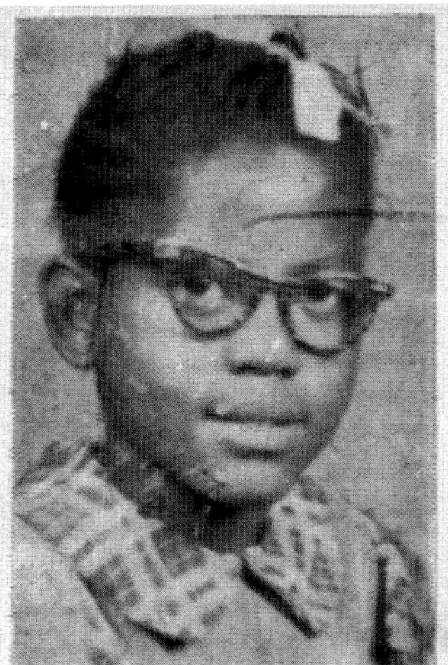
Addie Mae Collins

Cynthia Wesley

Cars in the general area were overturned and dented with rocks. Three that were parked near the church side entrance were knocked four feet backward by the explosion; sides of the almost-demolished vehicles were dotted with large holes, caused by flying debris. The church and nearby buildings were in shambles. The basement wall on the 16th Street side of the church was torn open, leaving a gaping hole. Just inside, the women's lounge was demolished.

Across 10th Street, the buildings in the black district were now windowless. Among the businesses damaged in the area were Social Cleaners, Jockey Boy Restaurant, Liberty Contracting Company, and Silver Sands Restaurant.

At the time of the explosion, the Rev. John Cross, then-pastor of Sixteenth Street Baptist Church, remembered being in the women's Bible study class, which met on the 16th Street side of the building.

"It was a wonderful lesson too, 'a love that forgives'. People seem to have love, but they don't know how to forgive," he told historian Horace Huntley in 1997 for the Birmingham Civil Rights Institute's Oral History Project.

"We'd been having difficulty with our hot-water heater in the kitchen area, and I thought it was the tank that had exploded down there. Then, in a few seconds, I didn't smell gas fumes, I smelled powder fumes. Immediately, I recognized that the hot-water heater didn't blow up, it was a bomb or something that went off.[12]

"There were some people that were injured, and they were being taken to the hospital.... I went around to look at the hole in the east side of the church. All I had to do was just bend over slightly and could walk right in.... We saw this bunch of debris there and they started digging down in there and less than two feet down we saw a body. We took that one out. They brought a stretcher in and dug down a little bit more and saw another one. So, they were all on top of each other, as if they had hugged each other."[13]

Ambulances moved in, then out with the injured and dead. Killed in the blast were 14-year-olds Cynthia Wesley, Carole Robertson, and Addie Mae Collins, and 11-year-old Denise

Juanita Jones, center, comforts her sister, Maxine McNair, whose daughter, Denise McNair, has been killed with three other girls the same day in the church bombing. At left is Clara Pippen, mother of the two women. The man at right is unidentified.

McNair. Besides killing the four girls, the explosion left nearly two dozen injured.

After the bodies were taken from the scene, Cross said officials heard what appeared to be moaning in the toilet stalls in the bomb-ravaged lounge. There they found 12-year-old Sarah Jean Collins, sister of Addie Mae.

"I didn't recognize who she was at the time, blood was streaming down her cheeks and she did seem incoherent," Cross said.[14]

Sarah suffered extensive damage to her left eye and spent more than eight weeks in the hospital.

Sarah, the youngest of the eight children of Arthur and Alice Collins, was very close to her sister, Addie Mae. "Everywhere you saw her, I was there. She was with me all the time," Sarah Collins-Rudolph told the *Birmingham Post-Herald* in a 1988 interview.[15]

Collins-Rudolph remembered being in a basement bathroom at the church with the other girls, preparing for a special youth program when the explosion demolished the side of the church.

"I was over at the sink and they were at the window.... That's why they got killed," Collins-Rudolph lamented.

She called out her sister's name and made her way out of the bathroom. "I couldn't see anything out of either one of my eyes," Collins-Rudolph said. "They called the ambulance, and they took me to the hospital."

She remained in the hospital until early November while doctors treated her eye injuries. She had to return to the hospital the next summer to have her right eye removed because it had become infected and the infection threatened to spread to her left eye.[16]

Collins-Rudolph said she cannot put the bombing too far from her mind.

"It's something that's sad," she told the *Birmingham Post-Herald* in 1988. "You go to church with your sister ... and the next minute you know you won't see your sister again because of somebody doing something terrible like that. I try not to think of it because it always hurts," she said. But she added, "I will never get over that feeling."

When the blast went off, Claude Wesley, 54, a principal at Lewis Elementary School, was having his car tank filled with gas. He abandoned the car and ran to the church but didn't find Cynthia. He went to University Hospital, where he was asked if the girl was wearing a ring. "I said, 'Yes.' " Wesley recalled. "They pulled her little hand out, and the little ring was there." [17]

Carolyn Maull McKinstry

McKinstry, 15 years old in 1963, had been a member of the Sixteenth Street Baptist Church since the age of two and was a secretary at the church. She offered this account of that awful September morning.[18]

"I always left home very early. My dad worked his second job on Sunday, and he would drop us off as he went to work. Normally, I took my sister to Sunday school with my two younger brothers and me. She wouldn't let me comb her hair that morning. I didn't want to take her anyway. So I told my mother, 'She won't let me comb her hair.' She said, 'OK, just go on without her.'

"So I took my brothers, and my dad dropped

Sixth Avenue Baptist Church is filled to capacity for the funeral of Denise, Cynthia and Addie Mae. More than 200 ministers attend and an estimated 600 people congregate inside and outside the church. Carole's funeral was held the day before.

us off. He was headed toward Mountain Brook. I assumed my duties as secretary. I had come through the downstairs area to pass out the attendance cards and the little envelopes where you record your money.

"I had done that and was heading back upstairs, when I saw the girls in the bathroom sort of laughing and talking and putting on their robes. They were excited. Actually, everybody was in Sunday school class, which is probably where they should have been, but they were excited.

"The phone rang. I answered the phone, and someone said, 'Two minutes.'

"Rev. Cross had not made us aware—maybe he made some of the adults aware—but a

The blast which damages the church also sends shockwaves around the world.

general announcement had not been made to the church that we had received bomb threats. I didn't know, didn't even think about what this might mean. The caller hung up. They said that, and then 'click.' I was just standing there and kind of thought about it, hung the phone up, and stepped out into the sanctuary because I had three or four more classes that I needed to give these cards to."

After the bombing, McKinstry said, "my first thoughts immediately were to find my two younger brothers.

"I could see that something had happened. I think I learned in that first minute or two that I was out there that our church had been bombed. Everybody was looking for somebody. I was looking for my two younger brothers and couldn't find them. They were in the Sunday school classes downstairs. So I went back downstairs, and I remember going into the boys' bathroom first, because I looked in all of the classrooms and I couldn't find them, so I went in the boys' bathroom, and I didn't see them there.

"Then I started in the girls' bathroom and I said, 'If they went to the bathroom, they probably wouldn't be in there.' But then they might, because they were little boys. They were, like, seven and five. So maybe they ran this way or maybe they just didn't know where to go. I spent a lot of time in the basement looking for them. I never found them, but my baby brother was found on Eighth Avenue, two blocks away.

"He had jumped out one of those side windows when it broke and just started running. I guess he ran with no real sense of where he was running, just knowing that he needed to get out of there. He just ran. Someone called my mom at home to tell her that they had bombed the church. When she was heading to the church to check on us, she encountered my baby brother.

"My dad found my oldest brother downtown. I guess a lot of kids just ran; they just scattered. I had been home about an hour and Mrs. [Alpha] Robertson called our house.

"She asked me did I see Carole. I said, 'No.' She asked to speak with my mom and just asked if she had seen her. She said, 'No.' She said, 'Maybe my Carole is all right. Your Carol is at home, so maybe my Carole is all right too.'"

McKinstry said she was constantly in fear.

"... I decided that I was probably going to be killed with one of these bombs. I was afraid. I was frightened. And it seemed there was no control. There was no way to stop what they were doing. There was no way to protect yourself. Helplessness is what I felt. I was so withdrawn after the church bombing. I did not attend the funeral of the four girls. I remember Mrs. Robertson calling. They were asking for some of us to be flower bearers at the funerals. I told my mom, 'Please don't make me go.' I was not sure what I would see.

"I knew I was really hurting inside and grieving that my friends were gone. I just did not want to be—I didn't want to see them. I didn't want to be there—part of that. She kept trying to encourage me to go. Finally, the day of the funeral, she called and said 'I think I'll let her stay here.' I didn't attend the funerals. I just didn't."[19]

Annetta Streeter Gary

Gary also remembered September 15, 1963.[20]

"When the church was bombed, it was like a dark cast on that day. Just looked like a gray day. It happened that Cynthia Wesley was in my sister's class. Denise McNair's father and my mother finished Tuskegee together. Carole Robertson's father was a music teacher at Washington Elementary School.

"My grandmother was a member of Sixteenth Street Baptist Church before her death, so I was familiar with the church and everything. It was a sad day. I attended the funerals along with my club members. We did not attend Carole's Robertson's funeral. We went to three funerals that were held together at Sixth Avenue Baptist Church."[21]

Virgil Ware

The bombing was not the only tragedy in Birmingham on September 15. Many members of the black community were shaken when they heard that 14-year-old Virgil Ware had died that day at the hands of two young white men, Michael Lee Farley and Larry Joe Sims.

Ware was killed on his way back from Docena, a community just outside Birmingham, where he and his brother James had gone to buy a bicycle for Virgil's paper route. They didn't find the bike at their uncle's scrap yard, so they rode back toward their home along Docena-Sandusky Road. That's when they encountered Farley and Sims.

Ware's brothers, James and Melvin, recalled the events of that day.[22]

James:

"When Virgil got shot, I really didn't know that [Sixteenth Street Baptist Church] had been bombed. I don't guess I knew anything until the next day. We left early that morning and went to (our) church, and I don't think we told anybody we were going to pick up the bike. We left early, and we stayed out there all day riding around. It was something like a junkyard more or less, just riding around on a bike. I didn't know anything about the church until the next day.

"That particular Sunday, we were on our way back. Virgil was on the handlebars, riding along. I was pulling him. I was bigger than all the rest of my siblings. They were little compared to me. I looked like my daddy. We saw a bike coming from the other direction [with two white boys on it]. We just kept pedaling. They got so close that they just overcame us.

"When Virgil got shot, he said. 'Wow, I'm shot.' He just fell off the handles and fell to the ground. I stood over him, and I guess five or six minutes later a car came by, and I told them what happened, and I told them where we stayed .... They turned around and brought my mom and dad and people down there. He was dead by that time. He didn't say anything after that, after he said, 'I'm shot.' He was fourteen, and I was sixteen."

Melvin:

"That day I was watching a football game. James and Virgil had gone to Docena to purchase a bicycle from my uncle. They flashed on the news about the bombing of the Sixteenth Street Baptist Church. I just shook.

"I was just about twelve, and my mind dawned on my brothers. I thought about their safety during that time. When they weren't back after about two p.m., I just walked and was tossing and turning. My mother had gone

Fourteen-year-old Virgil Ware is killed on Sept. 15, the same day as the four bombing victims. His body lies for years in an unmarked grave until family members and community activists hold a re-interment ceremony in 2005.

to the usher board, and when she had gotten back, a lady asked her if all of her children were home. She said, 'No, two of them are not at home.' The woman said, 'You better come with me.'

"That's when she went and found my two brothers. Virgil had been killed, and James was out there. The whole experience affected me deeply because it was like a piece of pie. You bake a pie, and then you take the pie out, you have a piece missing. That's really how it affected me. I thought about what Virgil would be doing now if he were still living. I would've liked to see him grown like us and have a family.

"It was real sad when I had to go back to school. My teachers and classmates had taken up some money to buy flowers at the funeral, and everybody gave their condolences and told you how sorry they were. It was sad ... I lost my brother over nothing.

"At the time, I thought it was all for nothing. But as time goes by, I believe it was for a reason. I believe there's a reason for everything. No question about it: that day launched the Civil Rights Movement with the bombing of the four girls and Virgil's death."

James:

"I remember the day my brother was shot 'cause I stayed there with Virgil so much. I don't even remember who stopped and went and got my mama and daddy. I believe those people were white. Anyway, they went and got my parents. When I went home, I didn't come out the house no more. I told the police what happened. That's all I did. I told them it was two guys (on a bike). The one on the back did the shooting. I had to testify at the trial.

"The first time I had seen [Farley and Sims] was at the trial. They had said at the time that they thought we had rocks. We didn't have anything. Virgil had both his hands on the handlebars, and it took all I had to pedal, so we didn't have anything. At the trial, that was never brought up. If it was, I don't remember. They asked me to point him out, and I pointed to the two guys. I never knew how the police found them that quick, I tell you the truth. When they came to my house, I remember [a detective] saying, 'I think we got a lead on who they were.' Next thing I know, we were at the grand jury, and they went on with the trial."

Farley and Sims were convicted of second-degree manslaughter and sentenced to seven months in jail, but a judge later reduced the sentence to probation because, in his words, "They came from good families," according to a report in the *Chicago Daily Defender.*[23]

"The verdict wasn't right. I figured they would have gotten more than what they did for what they did. To tell you the truth, I didn't expect them to catch them. Thank God that they did. I never thought they would. One (Farley) of them did call to apologize. He said, 'I want to apologize for what happened,' and he said, 'I know how it feels, I lost a nine-year-old son.' We didn't go into any details about it, though. I went on and accepted the apology because you can't go around hating the world. Let the Lord take care of that." [24]

The fallout

After the bombings and shootings, Birmingham took on the appearance of a battle zone, with 300 state troopers, 450 police officers, 150 sheriff's deputies, and 300 federalized National Guardsmen patrolling the streets. [25] Besides the four girls and Ware, another black, Johnny Robinson, had been shot in back by police on September 15 for throwing rocks to protest the church bombing. [25]

President Kennedy expressed "outrage" and "grief" one day after the bombing. In a statement, he said:

"I know I speak on behalf of all Americans in expressing a deep sense of outrage and grief over the killing of the children yesterday in Birmingham, Alabama. It is regrettable that public disparagement of law and order has encouraged violence which has fallen on the innocent. If these cruel and tragic events can only awaken that city and state—if they can only awaken this entire nation—to a realization of the folly of racial injustice and hatred and violence, then it is not too late for all concerned to unite in steps toward peaceful progress before more lives are lost."[26]

On Tuesday, September 17, a funeral was held for Carole Rosamond Robertson before 450 people, including 50 whites, at St. John's A.M.E. Church. The Rev. John Cross said the church bomber "did not only bomb the Sixteenth Street Baptist Church, did not only kill these lovely, innocent girls, but somehow the whole world was shaken. People everywhere died."

Words of the Apostle Paul were used as the text of Carole's eulogy.

Mr. and Mrs. Alvin Robertson grieve at a graveside service for their daughter Carole, who was killed in the bombing.

"All things work together for the good of them that love the Lord. Accept those words," Cross told Carole's family, seated in six pews just to the right of the pulpit. Carole's parents, Mr. and Mrs. Alvin Robertson, sat on the front row. She was their third child.[27]

On Wednesday, September 18, three coffins covered with floral arrangements were the focal point for a sea of somber faces that filled every available spot at Sixth Avenue Baptist Church. Funeral services for those three of the four girls crushed to death in the Sunday morning bombing just three days earlier, brought out a crowd that numbered in the thousands.

An hour before services began mourners and spectators were in balconies and Sunday school rooms. The main body of the church was reserved for families and friends of Cynthia Dianne Wesley, Addie Mae Collins, and Carol Denise McNair. Long after the 2,000-seat church was filled to capacity, people continued to crowd into the aisles and alongside corridors. More than 200 ministers, about half of them white, sat in a place reserved in the back of the church auditorium.[28]

An estimated crowd of 6,000 were inside and outside the church. Dr. Martin Luther King Jr. speaking from the black-cloth-draped pulpit, called the girls "the modern heroines of a holy crusade."

He said, "We must not harbor the desire to retaliate with violence. We must not lose faith with our white brothers."

Dr. King predicted the deaths "may well serve as the redemptive force that brings light to this dark city ... may cause the white South to come to terms with its conscience."[29]

After the service, an estimated 4,000 people outside the church watched as the coffins and families emerged into the late-afternoon sunlight, one at a time. The three hearses moved away slowly through the masses, the people parting to let them and the families through. Cynthia and Addie Mae were buried in Woodlawn Cemetery; Denise at Shadow Lawn Cemetery, where her friend, Carole, had been buried that Tuesday.[30]

OCTOBER TO DECEMBER 1963

Birmingham's Moment Of Crisis:

A Statement Of Concern And Conviction

We, the undersigned Citizens of Birmingham, are convinced that the time has come for us to say these things clearly:

1. The Negro members of this community believe that we are now in a period of crisis as great as any we have known. The unhampered criminal acts that have been recently perpetrated against us—cause us grave concern.

Our churches and homes have been bombed, and no one has been charged with one act of bombing. Our children have been wounded and killed, and no murderer has been convicted. Therefore, we fear for our lives and the lives of our families. We are forced to stand guard at our homes.

Negro Citizens find it extremely difficult to trust the agents of law enforcement—local, state or federal; and all too often they have come to feel that resort to the courts has resulted in justice delayed and, in many cases, justice denied.

2. At this urgent moment we believe that strong, fearless, immediate action on the part of our city government is absolutely necessary.

The protection of its citizens and the allaying of their just fears is the responsibility of any government, and the government of Birmingham must not allow threats of reprisal nor unnecessary bureaucratic machinery to stand in the way of its clear and present duty.

3. Both the grave concerns and the firm convictions stated above are shared by the vast majority of Birmingham's Negro citizens. We are not satisfied with a life of constant intimidation, segregation and fear, nor have we ever been. No human being is.

Therefore, we the undersigned, are all proud to endorse and support the leadership of our friends, Martin Luther King, Jr., and Fred Shuttlesworth, in our common struggle to make Birmingham a better place for all of its citizens. We do not consider these men outsiders to our cause. (Indeed, Rev. Shuttlesworth voted in the last municipal election, and pays taxes in this City and County.)

So, we affirm that Dr. King and Rev. Shuttlesworth are our leaders; their goals are ours, our struggle is theirs.

4. Standing together with these men, in the present moment of crisis, we are convinced that there is one logical first step the city of Birmingham must take now: hire a substantial number of Negro policemen for duty in this city. If, in their assigned districts, these men are given the same authority as all other officers of their rank, their presence will make a great difference to us. It will bring to us a greater confidence in the local police force and a greater sense of safety.

Indeed, we are certain that the presence of Negro officers will help convince many persons that they no longer need to depend on their own resources for protection, nor turn to violence in search of justice. The morale of Birmingham's Negro citizens is at least as important as the morale of its police force.

5. We believe that such action by the city is a reasonable first step—but only a first step. For Birmingham has much unfinished business in the difficult undertaking of making basic constitutional rights available to all of its citizens, without regard to race.

Therefore, we are still convinced that action must come in the immediate future on such issues as: removal of racial signs on city-owned premises; employment of Negroes in all tax-supported municipal offices; desegregation of all public facilities, including hospitals; and desegregation of those private facilities serving the public.

These steps cover only the minimum distance that we must travel to a reign of justice in our city. Because Birmingham is our home, we pledge our lives and our fortunes to this cause, promising to persevere in this pilgrimage until we have reached the goal of "liberty and justice for all!"

Atty. Arthur D. Shores
Dr. and Mrs. J. T. Montgomery
Bishop E. P. Murchison
John J. Drew
Dr. Joel S. Boykins
L. S. Gaillard, Jr.
Herschell L. Hamilton, M.D.
Rev. Harold D. Long
Rev. Abraham Woods, Jr.
Rev. Edward Gardner
Atty. Oscar Adams, Jr.
Lucinda B. Robey
Mrs. Bernice Johnson
Rev. John Thomas Porter
Mrs. Katie Jefferson
W. H. Hollins
Atty. Orzell Billingsley, Jr.
Mrs. Ruth J. Jackson
Mrs. Willa G. Adams
R. C. Stewart, M.D.
Mrs. G. A. Curry
Samuel Taylor
Depew E. Bradford, M.D.
Mrs. L. S. Gaillard, Jr.
Clinton Moon
S. E. Welch, D.D.S.
V. L. Harris
Mrs. Lessie M. Smith
Betty Hill

Atty. George S. White
Rev. N. H. Smith, Jr.
C. J. Greene
Rev. J. H. Calloway
B. M. Jefferson, D.D.S.
Franke Dukes
Eddie Upshaw
Rev. Joseph Ellwanger
Rev. J. E. Robinson
Rev. L. J. Rogers
Clarence Whisenant
Alan Hirsch
Rev. A. D. William King
Rev. Nathaniel Linsey
Mrs. Addine Drew
Tyree J. Barefield-Pendleton, M.D.
Mrs. Ruth Barefield-Pendleton
John A. Poole
Mrs. Joel S. Boykins
Mrs. Lillian Stone Moore
A. W. Plump, M.D.
Mrs. A. W. Plump
Mrs. G. R. Lee
Maurice W. Ryles
W. E. Sterling, Sr.
Mr. and Mrs. Ernest E. Gibson
Rev. John H. Cross
Jessie J. Lewis
James Johnson

Willie G. Rucker
Samuel Oneal
Mr. and Mrs. L. S. Gaillard, Sr.
Mrs. Dester Brooks
Miss Annie Peterson
W. C. Patton, Jr.
Miss Catherine Hollins
A. F. Bonner, Jr.
H. McCain
E. H. Griffins
Preston Evans
P. L. Evans
M. L. Forniss
Mrs. Myrtis Dowdell
Mr. R. L. Dowdell
Alfonso W. Hawkins
Mrs. N. J. Lumzy
Mrs. Rosie Lee McDuffie
Mr. R. L. Lumzy
Mrs. Minnie L. Cook
John Williams
Matthew Robinson
Mrs. L. V. Hale
James E. Freeman
Robert C. Hester
James Cade
Percy Bell, Jr.
Katie Patrick
Mr. and Mrs. Willie R. Parry

Mrs. Maggie L. Hawkins
Willie Ruth Crusoe
John Banks
Mrs. Mary Franklin
Alex Combs
William R. Sherman
Ronald C. Hatcher
A. G. Gaston, Jr.
James Armstrong
Mr. & Mrs. Sylvester Harris
Atty. Peter A. Hall
John W. Gillespie
Julia Gillespie
Willard Hill
Mabel Jean Adam
Thomas E. Wrean
Rev. C. H. George
Mrs. C. S. George
Mrs. H. G. Heath
October W. Heath
Jonathan McPherson
Rev. L. H. Welchel, Jr.
Rev. C. W. Woods
Samuel E. Harris, M.D.
Atty. Demetrus C. Newton
Rev. L. S. Brannon
Georgia W. Price

October to December 1963

Healing from a volatile September, deciding whether to hire black police officers, and mourning a slain president marked some of the highlights in the final three months of the year for Birminghamians.

On Sunday, October 6, eighty-eight mostly white civic leaders and residents published a full-page ad in *The Birmingham News* asking the mayor and city council to contemplate hiring black police officers. The ad began:

> "For many years the use of Negro policemen has been discussed by the citizens and former city officials of Birmingham. Negro policemen have been and are successfully employed in many Southern communities, including cities in Alabama. Their services have been particularly valuable in the enforcement of law and order in the Negro communities in which they serve."

The group asked that immediate consideration be given to the hiring of Negro policemen "subject to conditions."[1] Those included that a "Negro precinct be established in the Negro community for duty in that area;" that "the personnel board promptly advertise for applicants to take the required qualifying examination for specific duty in the Negro districts;" that "the Negro precinct operate under the authority vested in the Chief of Police of the City of Birmingham;" and that the program be "implemented without delay and completed within six months."

Two weeks later, on Sunday, October 20, one hundred and sixteen black residents published a full-page ad in *The Birmingham News*, titled "Birmingham's Moment of Crisis: A Statement of Concern and Conviction." Signed by attorneys Arthur D. Shores, Oscar Adams Jr., Orzell Billingsley Jr., and George S. White, and more than three dozen pastors, including those from some of the city's largest congregations, the ad began:

> "The Negro members of this community believe that we are now in a period of crisis as great as any we have known. The unhampered criminal acts that have been recently perpetrated against us cause us grave concern.
>
> "Our churches and homes have been bombed, and no one has been charged with one act of bombing. Our children have been wounded and killed, and no murderer has been convicted. Therefore, we fear for our lives and the lives of our families. We are forced to stand guard at our homes.
>
> "Negro citizens find it extremely difficult to trust the agents of law enforcement—local, state, or federal; and all too often they have come to feel that resorting to the courts has resulted in justice delayed and, in many cases, justice denied."

The citizens who purchased the ad asked city leaders to take action in several areas, including removal of racist signs on city-owned premises; employment of Negroes in all tax-supported municipal offices; desegregation of all public facilities, including hospitals; and desegregation of private facilities that serve the public. The last paragraph of the ad said:

> "These steps cover only the minimum distance that we must travel to a reign of justice in our city. Because Birmingham is our home, we pledge our lives and our fortunes to this cause, promising to persevere in this pilgrimage until we have reached the goal of 'liberty and justice for all!' "

On Tuesday, October 22, city officials rejected proposals for hiring black policemen. The three-member city council public safety committee issued a preliminary report, which said that in the face of present civil service laws "we cannot recommend that anyone be employed as a matter of special privilege only."[2] Mayor Boutwell, who had final responsibility for hiring city personnel, concurred.

In a statement, Boutwell said:

> "My complete support of a strong and impartial civil service system, created to give the city the very best possible employees in all its departments and to guarantee full protections of those employees after they have earned permanent status is well-known and long-standing," he said. "The methods of hiring public employees are not and cannot be dictated by individuals or groups. It is dictated purely by good and effective laws which have provided to this city as fine a staff of municipal employees as any city in the nation."[3]

On Friday, November 22, President Kennedy was slain by an assassin's bullet in Dallas. On Monday, November 25, Birmingham city offices and churches joined in final formal tribute. Public offices and schools were closed. Flags flew at half staff, their red, white, and blue, bold against the somber sky. Memorial services were held in churches and temples. [4]

At 11 a.m., as television cameras allowed all of America to attend the president's funeral, Birmingham was quiet. Many local churches held special prayer and communion services at the hour the ceremony was conducted in St. Matthew's Cathedral in Washington, D.C.

Several Birmingham churches expressed sympathy in the wake of Kennedy's assassination. Both black and white clergy tried to console, and to put the national loss in perspective.

"This death of President Kennedy has caused a shadow of despondence to envelope the hopes and aspirations of many people throughout the world," said the Rev. J.L. Ware, pastor of Trinity Baptist Church and president of the Birmingham Baptist Ministers Conference [5]

The Rev. Edward Gardner, pastor of Mt. Olive Baptist Church and First Vice-President of the Alabama Christian Movement of Human Rights said, "We have lost one of our greatest presidents of the United States since the days of Abraham Lincoln. I also consider the Negro group has lost a great friend, Mr. John F. Kennedy." [6]

The Rev. John H. Cross, pastor of the recently bombed Sixteenth Street Baptist Church, said, "The audacious act which took the life of President John F. Kennedy was a shock to the whole

EXTRA The Birmingham News EXTRA

76th Year—No. 254 | 38 Pages—2 Sections | Birmingham, Ala., Friday, November 22, 1963 | Price: 5 Cents

PRESIDENT IS ASSASSINATED; LYNDON JOHNSON SWORN IN

Shock, disbelief grip Magic City

Shock . . . grief . . . condemnation . . . disapproval . . . dismay . . .

These were among the man-on-the-street's reactions in downtown Birmingham Friday afternoon minutes after official announcement of President Kennedy's assassination in Dallas, Tex.

Businessmen followed developments on car and transistor radios. Others gathered near television sets. Others huddled in small sidewalk caucuses.

American flags were at half-mast all over the city.

Of the dozen persons polled at random by The Birmingham News, five refused to comment or have their picture taken. One man emphasized his objection to publicity by grabbing at a camera.

The first person questioned, Mrs. Ruby [illegible], a waitress at the Bankhead Hotel dining room, said, "I think it's the most tragic thing that ever happened to the United States. It shook up everybody in the lunch room. They couldn't eat."

TEARS STAINING her cheeks, Joan Wallace, 116 Hardy Road, said, "I think it's terrible. He just died you know. I didn't like him, but I didn't want him to die."

State Rep. Walter Emmett Perry Jr. broke away from a conversation near 20th Street and said:

"Assassination is something that had not occurred in many years. Assassination is something that we had all thought to [illegible]

"I think security must have been very sloppy. Not only the President's death but permitting the vice president to ride in the same parade," Perry said. "God bless the President. God bless Lyndon Johnson."

The next man, waiting for a traffic light, said, "It's just too bad, but I'd rather you not publish my picture." He also withheld his name.

"It has to be a terrible thing," said A. E. Brown, 1129 Lay Drive. "I don't advocate an assassination. But we needed a new President."

THE NEXT PERSON inter-

Turn to Page 4, Column 4

PRESIDENT LYNDON JOHNSON . . . Vice-President until today

Johnson sworn in, takes off for capital

DALLAS, Nov. 22—(AP)—Lyndon B. Johnson was sworn in as President of the United States at about 2:30 p.m. (CST) today.

The oath was administered by U. S. District Judge Sarah T. Hughes.

Johnson took the oath aboard the presidential plane at Dallas' Love Field. He was preparing to fly to Washington to take over the government.

This is the presidential oath: "I do solemnly swear that I will faithfully execute the office of President of the United States, and will to the best of my ability, preserve, protect and defend the Constitution of the United States."

FURTHER DETAILS of the swearing in were not immediately available.

Present at the swearing-in were Mrs. Kennedy and Mrs. Johnson, several staff members and several congressmen.

Johnson asked as many of the White House people as possible to crowd into the executive suite of the plane to witness the ceremony.

Judge Hughes wept as she administered the presidential oath to Johnson.

The presidential plane took off immediately for Washington with Johnson, Mrs. Johnson and Mrs. Kennedy and some White House aides aboard.

At 6 feet 3, weighing close to 200 pounds, Johnson has always been supercharged with energy.

He has been called self-centered and considerate; a humanitarian and power-hungry; a shrewd opportunist and a political genius; tough and yet vulnerable; vain, friendly, sensitive, flamboyant.

FRIENDS AND others who watched him on his rise over the decades agreed that he was just flexible enough, or human enough, to have been all of those things at one time or another.

Johnson once said of himself:

"I am a free man, an American, a United States senator, and a Democrat, in that order.

"I am also a liberal, a conservative, a Texan, a taxpayer, a rancher, a business man, a consumer, a parent, a voter, and not as young as I used to be nor as old as I expect to be—and I am all those things in no fixed order."

Arthur Edson, Associated Press writer who has specialized on politics and personalities, once commented that a person's opinion of Johnson would be swayed by where that person met him. He wrote, on the basis of personal knowledge of Johnson in all his phases:

A SENATE majority leader, he was all over the political scene but some thought he would have to slow down when he became vice president—ordinarily just a ceremonial job.

But he took on so many chores he needed three offices from which to operate—in the Capitol, in the new Senate office building and in the White House. He kept 17 staffers hopping.

Johnson, who was Kennedy's vice president, automatically succeeded to the presidency.

LEE H. OSWALD, 24, ARRESTED SCREAMING IN THEATER AFTER JFK KILLED . . . Dallas police said he was arrested in connection with slaying of a Dallas policeman, and was being questioned about assassination of President Kennedy.

Man held in assassination, slaying of cop

DALLAS, Nov. 22—(AP)—A 24-year-old man who said two years ago he wanted Russian citizenship was questioned today to see whether he had any connection with the assassination of President Kennedy.

He was identified as Lee Harvey Oswald of Fort Worth. He was pulled screaming and yell-

Turn to Page 4, Column 5

No market report

The New York and American stock exchanges closed today upon word of the assassination of President Kennedy, so today's Red Star final of The News does not carry the customary closing market reports.

Governor deplores 'act of malice'

HALEYVILLE, Nov. 22—Gov. George C. Wallace said that whoever shot President John F. Kennedy and Texas Gov. John Connally "must be filled with universal malice toward all."

In Haleyville to dedicate a new high school, the governor made the following statement when noti- [illegible]

"We are saddened by the news we have heard that the President and Gov. Connally have been shot. I was with Gov. Connally in White Sulphur Springs, W. Va., at a recent Southern Governor's Conference and became well acquainted with him.

"It is hard to believe that anyone would shoot at the President of the United States. It is the same as if they had shot at you and at me.

"I may have differed with the President on political matters but this is a terrible thing and I pray that the next news we hear will be good.

"WHAT ARE WE COMING to in this country when our President [illegible] of a city like Dallas in safety.

"Whoever did this terrible thing must be filled with universal malice toward all."

LIEUTENANT GOVERNOR James B. Allen of Gadsden:

"Alabama joins the rest of the nation and the entire world in being shocked and distressed at the cowardly blows dealt President Kennedy and Gov. Connally. All political considerations should be brushed aside and all should join in prayers for the recover of the President and Gov. Connally. During the time the President's life hangs in the balance, certainly there should be a moratorium on advocacy or opposition to civil

Turn to Page 4, Column 1

Sniper cuts down JFK in Dallas

DALLAS, Nov. 22—(AP)—A furtive sniper armed with a high-powered rifle assassinated President John F. Kennedy today. Barely two hours after Kennedy's death, Lyndon B. Johnson took the oath of office as the 37th President of the United States.

Kennedy was shot through the head and neck as he rode through Dallas in the presidential limousine in what had been a triumphal motorcade.

When the shots were fired at about 12:30 p.m. CST and the chief executive slumped forward, Mrs. Kennedy turned in the seat ahead of him and cried, "Oh, no," in anguish and horror.

She tried to cradle his head in her arms as the limousine took off at top speed for Parkland Hospital where Kennedy died about half an hour later.

Kennedy, who was 46, was cut down by a flurry of bullets shortly after his open-topped car had left the Dallas business district, where thousands had massed 10 to 12 deep along each curb to cheer him and Mrs. Kennedy.

This was the first presidential assassination since 1901 when a half-crazed gunman shot William McKinley at close range during a reception in Buffalo, N. Y.

KENNEDY WAS the first president to die in office since Franklin D. Roosevelt succumbed to a cerebral hemorrhage in April, 1945.

The Secret Service, the Federal Bureau of Investigation and Dallas police swung into action within seconds and launched what was perhaps the biggest, determined manhunt in the nation's history.

A number of suspects were picked up during the next few hours.

GOV. JOHN CONNALLY of Texas, also wounded by the sniper, was described this afternoon as being in "very, very serious but not critical" condition.

Julian Read, an aide to Connally, said Connally suffered three wounds . . . one in the right arm, one in the right leg and one in the back that pierced his body.

KENNEDY WAS administered the last rites of the Roman Catholic Church shortly after he was carried into Parkland Hospital. He was the nation's first Catholic president.

Emergency treatment given the dying president was described for newsmen by two physicians, Drs. Kemp Clark, 38, and Malcolm Perry, 34.

Dr. Perry said Kennedy suffered a neck wound—a bullet hole in the lower part of the neck. There was a second wound in Kennedy head, but Perry was not certain whether it was inflicted by the same bullet.

THE PHYSICIAN said the President lost consciousness as soon as he was hit and never revived.

"We never had any hope of saving his life," said Perry, though eight of 10 physicians attended him in a frantic but futile effort to keep Kennedy alive.

Clark, a brain surgeon, reported that Kennedy was given oxygen and blood transfusions, then was administered an anaesthetic as surgeons cut a hole in the President's windpipe in an attempt to ease his breathing.

Perry said that shortly after he reached the hospital, the chief executive's heart action failed and "there was no palpable pulse beat."

The time of death was announced officially as 1 p.m., CST.

POLICE BELIEVED the fatal volley was fired from a textbook warehouse overlooking the expressway down which the president's car was heading.

Bob Jackson, a photographer for the Dallas Times Herald, heard one shot, then two rapid burst as he rode in an open convertible in the presidential motorcade.

He said he looked up and saw two men peering from an upper-story window of the warehouse. As he looked, he said, he saw a rifle being drawn quickly back into a sixth floor window.

Police began a massive search of the big structure, emptying it of all employes.

Automatically, the mantle of the Presidency fell to Vice President Lyndon B. Johnson, a native Texan who had been riding two cars behind the chief executive.

The First Lady cradled her dying husbands' blood-smeared head in her arms as the presidential limousine raced to the hospital.

"Oh, no," she kept crying.

Connally slumped in his seat beside the President.

Police ordered an unprecedented dragnet of the city, hunting for the assassin.

They believed the fatal shots were fired by a white man about 30, slender of build, weighing about 165 pounds, and standing 5 feet 10 inches tall.

Even as two clergymen hovered over the fallen President in the hospital emergency room, doctors and nurses administered blood transfusions.

Kennedy died of a gunshot wound in the brain at approximately 1 p.m., according to an announcement by acting White House Press Secretary Malcolm Kilduff.

The new President, Lyndon Johnson, and his wife left the hospital a half hour later. Newsmen had no opportunity to question them.

THE HORROR OF the assassination was mirrored in an eyewitness account by Sen. Ralph Yarbrough, D-Tex., who had been riding three cars behind Kennedy.

"You could tell something awful and tragic had happened," the senator told newsmen before Kennedy's death became known. His voice breaking and his eyes red-rimmed, Yarborough said:

"I could see a Secret Service man in the President's car leaning on the car with his hands in anger, anguish and despair. I knew then something tragic had happened."

Yarborough had counted three rifle shots as teh presidential limousine left downtown Dallas through a triple underpass. The shots were fired from above—possibly from one of the bridges or from a nearby building.

ONE WITNESS, television reporter Mal Couch, said he saw a gun emerge from an upper story of a warehouse commanding an unobstructed view of the presidential car.

Kennedy and his wife had just passed the halfway point in a three-day speaking tour through Texas.

The President already had prepared a luncheon address for a Dallas audience before he died. In his prepared text, he assailed his ultra-conservative critics.

DALLAS IS CONSIDERED a center of conservative philosophy and finance.

Here, on Oct. 24, Adlai E. Stevenson was spat upon by [illegible]

Turn to Page 4, Column 1

PRESIDENT, TEXAS GOVERNOR GUNNED DOWN, SECRET SERVICE MEN LOOK WHERE SHOT CAME FROM . . . President Kennedy critically wounded today as motorcade left downtown Dallas, Tex.

world. We have lost a leader and a champion for the cause of human freedom."[7]

The Rev. Abraham Woods, Jr., pastor of First Metropolitan Baptist Church and second vice-president of the ACMHR, said, "November 22, 1963, will indeed be recorded as one of the blackest Fridays in the annals of history.... The world has lost a great statesman, this nation has lost a great leader, and oppressed, exploited, and deprived people everywhere, people who yearn to breathe the invigorating air of freedom, justice, and equality have lost a great friend and benefactor."[8]

At a solemn requiem mass in Birmingham's St. Paul's Cathedral, Monsignor Francis Wade read these prepared remarks:

> "President Kennedy was the victim of extremism—an extremism which coming from the right and left is squeezing out the blood of our national life and unity. It is an extremism that most often finds expression in unreasonableness, in half-truths, in acrimony, in invective, in bitterness, in rumor and unfounded charges—and even sometimes in hate that turns to violence."[9]

At memorial services in Canterbury Methodist Church in Mountain Brook, Dr. Allen Montgomery told more than 500 people:

> "[John F. Kennedy was] the symbol of America, just as the Stars and Stripes and the mighty eagle that together express what we mean when we say America. We memorialize a fallen leader ... a citizen, a patriot, a father, and a husband. We share in the grief of all to whom he was personally dear. One day history will render a verdict on the 35th president of the United States. And then, perhaps not until then, will the nation truly realize how great was our loss on November 22, 1963."[10]

The death of a president left Birmingham as stunned as the rest of the nation as 1963 approached its end. But ordinary life went on in Birmingham, where the final month of the year

From left: The Rev. Abraham Woods; the Rev. Ed Gardner; the Rev. John H. Cross. The ministers pay respects in their churches when President John F. Kennedy is slain.

was marked by a civic project, a fire tragedy and weather related events:

On Thursday, December 12, state officials announced an agreement to begin immediate construction of a Red Mountain Expressway bridge over 21st Street, along with an offer from Birmingham to pay matching funds to extend the expressway two additional blocks into the city. A decision to begin the $14.7 million second-phase construction of the thoroughfare was expected to be reached by city and county officials.[11]

On Monday, December 23, six black children, ranging in age from seven months to six years, died in a fire that raged through their Collegeville home. The children were trapped in the rear of their six-room brick-veneer house when a pile of clothing caught near a hot-water heater at the back of the structure caught fire. Officers said the flames blocked the back door, which was the only means of escape.[12]

Firemen said the children retreated as far as they could go. Three of them were in the bathroom, and the others were just outside. The whole interior was burned, and apparently the furnishings were a total loss. The fire spread rapidly, scorching the walls and ceilings throughout the house. The parents were reported to be at work when the blaze occurred, according to investigators.[13]

On Christmas Day, a 14-year-old Woodlawn High School student missing for two days was found frozen to death in an open ditch near Eastwood Mall. The death was from a fall and exposure to the elements, although an autopsy was ordered.[14]

The year 1963 ended with a surprise coating of snow that closed many roads; accumulation in some areas of the city reached eight inches. State troopers reported that all arteries into Birmingham were impassable without chains on tires. U.S. Highway 280 South was practically blocked to any vehicles. Both bus lines serving Birmingham suspended operations. All flights in and out of Municipal Airport were canceled around midnight. The evening New Year's Eve shift of the Birmingham Police Department investigated 66 accidents, though no fatalities were reported. And the Birmingham Transit Co. said it was operating "as many buses as possible."[15]

Thus closed a year consumed by turmoil caused by civil rights demonstrations, public school integration, and tragic bombings.

Epilogue

On January 1, 1964, *The Birmingham News* published a nearly-6,000-word front-page editorial reflecting on the "Trials and Blessings of 1963," in which the newspaper asked future generations:

> "Did the older folks make the tough but right decisions in 1963—did they carry them out in year after year that followed? Did we serve you youngsters—our children—by putting you ahead of our own personal wishes or prejudices or desires? Did we pay the price for your future?" [1]

Fifty years later, the verdict is in.

"Looking back at 1963—the rigid segregation that existed and the exclusion of blacks from entire categories of public- and private-sector jobs—there simply has been a huge social transformation that has allowed there to be a degree of community, regardless of race, that would have been absolutely unimaginable back then," says Edward Shannon LaMonte, retired Birmingham-Southern College professor of political science.

Since 1963, Birmingham has elected four black mayors, appointed three black police chiefs, and installed seven black school superintendents. Still, much work remains to be done in the city, according to LaMonte and others.

"There are serious social, political, and economic problems in Birmingham. But if you look over the 50-year span between 1963 and the present, there have been fundamental transitions in each of these three broad areas of community life," explains LaMonte, who also served as the former director of the University of Alabama at Birmingham Center for Urban Affairs, and as a senior staff person in the administration of Richard Arrington, Birmingham's first black mayor.

Jefferson County Circuit Judge Helen Shores Lee grew up in Birmingham as the daughter of prominent civil rights attorney Arthur Shores. She acknowledges the changes in the city, but also points out that some problems linger.

"Prejudice and social injustice still exist in this city, and they play a role in terms of the opportunities people enjoy today," Lee says. "Jim Crow laws may not exist anymore, but the spirit of Jim Crow is alive and well, primarily due to institutional racism, which often makes it difficult for us recognize it and root it out.

"We certainly need more diversity training in our various institutions," Lee continues. "We have won legislative victories, of course. I have learned over my 65-plus years that people's thoughts can't be legislated. The secret hates and prejudices of their hearts are not bridled by any laws. Many of those attitudes that were there in the 60s still prevail."

Health care is one area in which blacks in Birmingham are still treated unfairly, Lee says.

"There is a disparity in the emergency room

treatment that blacks receive versus that received by whites," Lee explains. "We have seen research, and a large part of what the University of Alabama is doing through its Minority Health Research Center is trying to eliminate racial disparities in health care."

Lee adds that national reports of restrictions on voter registration and identification laws, in addition to questions about the constitutionality of immigration laws, raise concerns about racial equality even today.

Jim Rotch, a partner in the Birmingham law firm Bradley Arant Boult & Cummings LLP, and creator of The Birmingham Pledge, agrees that the community can still mature.

"We've made very significant strides over the past 50 years," Rotch says. "Are we where we need to be? Absolutely not. We're certainly moving in the right direction and making significant strides, though."

The Birmingham Pledge, written in 1998, calls upon individuals to commit to fight racism and prejudice; to recognize the basic dignity of all individuals, regardless of race or color; and to act on these principles daily. The Pledge has been signed by South African activist and Nobel Prize winner Archbishop Desmond Tutu, former U.S. President Bill Clinton, U.S. Secretary of State Hillary Clinton, and more than 122,000 people worldwide.

The Pledge, according to Rotch, encourages people to discuss the issue of race, which has been difficult for some, given Birmingham's ugly past.

"Even today, there are a lot of people who think that if we just quit talking about racial problems they'll go away," Rotch says. "Very good people, very well-intentioned people, who don't consider themselves racially prejudiced, believe that if we just quit talking about it, then it will go away. I have never been able to agree with that point of view.

"Not talking about racial problems doesn't make them go away," he says, comparing such problems to a deadly disease—cancer. "If you don't acknowledge that you have cancer and don't do something to get rid of it, the disease will grow until it destroys you. I think race is much the same way."

Fifty years ago, some Birmingham residents initiated a Movement to rid the cancer of racism from the community, and those efforts came at a cost. But it wasn't the "older folks" that "paid the price for the future," as *The Birmingham News* suggested in its New Year's Day 1964 editorial. The foot soldiers and those who supported the Movement are the ones who paid the real price, says Lee, who co-wrote, with her sister Barbara Shores, a book about their father, *The Gentle Giant of Dynamite Hill.*

"Let's take the children's march," Lee said. "Think about the teachers who turned their heads so the kids could go out of the doors to participate in that demonstration, knowing that doing so openly could have cost them their jobs. Or the parents that were fearful for their children participating in such a march, but, at the same time, were proud that they participated. It was a good feeling to do that. You felt that you were doing something really important—important to the state, important to the country."

Lee recalls that many of the children were determined to make life better for future generations. "It wasn't right to have persons of color barred from certain institutions or stores or lunch counters," Lee says. "That whole sit-in movement and the boycott sparked change with a lot of our stores and companies, but it took guts to do that. The fear was there all the time that something bad could happen, and some of those young kids were hurt when targeted by fire hoses and dogs.

"Many of them were injured, but that didn't stop them. It was as if there was a revelation in their hearts that said, 'We don't want to continue to grow up like this and be denied, and be told what we can and cannot do.' "

Freeman A. Hrabowski III, who grew up in Birmingham's Titusville neighborhood and attended Ullman High School, was one of the child marchers. He was jailed for five days at age 12 for taking part in that civil rights protest. Hrabowski, a widely respected author and educator, was named in 2012 one of *Time* magazine's Top 100 Most Influential People in the World. He has served since 1992 as president of the University of Maryland, Baltimore County, an institution with students from 150 countries.

"There is no doubt that the 1963 marches and the attention they brought to Birmingham, coupled with the tragedy of the four little girls that September, led to more light shining on the segregated world in which we lived and the problems with segregation," Hrabowski says. "I learned that even children really could make a difference in their own lives. That march empowered us to understand that we could do something that would have the country thinking about how children should be treated.

"Those efforts, those activities, and what happened afterward led to major concessions in our city. And for the first time, the message was that America did not have to be as it had been. Just because things were one way didn't mean they had to always be that way. If you've always seen people at the bottom, you tend to think that's where they are supposed to be, and the people themselves even tend to think that way.

"The message from Dr. King and others ... was that we could be the best in the country, 'Not the best Negro children, but the best.' And the march was symbolic of that."

Most historians agree that 1963 was a necessary step toward equal rights for people, not just in Birmingham but across Alabama, throughout the United States, and around the world.

"The trauma of 1963 was a prerequisite for the change that came later because the sources of resistance were so numerous and so entrenched that there had to be a profound disruption in order to bring about significant change," LaMonte says.

Rotch calls the Civil Rights Movement a watershed moment in history.

"You can argue about who played the biggest role—whether it was Rosa Parks on the bus in Montgomery, whether it was Bull Connor with the dogs and the fire hoses, whether it was the bombing of the church," he says. "But I don't think there is any question that, but for Birmingham, we wouldn't be where we are today and making progress in civil rights."

The Rev. Anderson Williams, pastor of New Shady Grove Missionary Baptist Church in Birmingham (Rising), remembers when he couldn't sit at the lunch counters and had to drink from a water fountain marked "Colored."

"Looking back, the progress that we've made is tremendous—and we owe it all to God," says Williams, who grew up in segregated Birmingham and was among the first black bus drivers in the city. "God was always in the plan and at the forefront of what was going on. The revolution really started in the Christian faith. Dr. King, the churches in this city came together.

"What we were going through sort of reminded me of the children of Israel. Black people were in bondage and had to go through a period of preparation in order to recognize and realize the blessing that God had bestowed upon us. We still have not accomplished all we can accomplish, but we have come a long way. And it's only through the grace of God that we are as far along as we are."

1963 Timeline

11 **JANUARY, FRIDAY**
Contracts signed to begin construction of the multimillion-dollar Red Mountain Expressway; the first phase of the project will take 15–18 months to complete.

14 **JANUARY, MONDAY**
George C. Wallace takes over as Alabama governor. During his inaugural he calls for "segregation now … segregation tomorrow … segregation forever!"

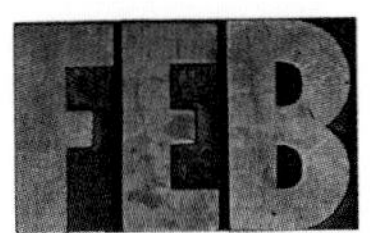

15 **FEBRUARY, FRIDAY**
An injunction petition is filed against the Birmingham Election Commission in Circuit Court to halt the upcoming March 5 Birmingham election.

20 **FEBRUARY, WEDNESDAY**
Birmingham Mayor **Arthur J. Hanes** loses his bid to stop the March 5 mayor-council city election.

5 **MARCH, TUESDAY**
In the mayoral election, former Alabama Lt. Gov. **Albert Boutwell** receives 39 percent of the vote and Birmingham Commissioner of Public Safety Theophilus Eugene "Bull" Connor receives 31 percent, setting up an April 2 runoff.

24 **MARCH, SUNDAY**
A heavy explosion heard over much of Birmingham destroys a black residence, injuring at least two people and damaging houses and other buildings over a two-block radius.

31 **MARCH, SUNDAY**
Birmingham Transit Co. operators and maintenance workers vote to go on strike; the Amalgamated Association of Street, Electric, Railway, and Motor Coach Employees of America, Division 725 vote 274 to 117 in favor of the strike.

2 APRIL, TUESDAY

Boutwell decisively defeats Connor in the mayoral race; unofficial returns from the city's 151 boxes show that Boutwell takes 29,630 votes to 21,648 for Connor.

3 APRIL, WEDNESDAY

The Alabama Christian Movement for Human Rights (ACMHR) and the Southern Christian Leadership Council (SCLC) lead sit-in demonstrations at downtown Birmingham lunch counters; twenty participants are arrested at Britt's lunch counters, while Kress, Loveman's, Pizitz, and Woolworth's close their counters.

5 APRIL, FRIDAY

Ten sit-in demonstrators are arrested, including six at Lane Drugstore (First Avenue and 20th Street) and four at Tutwiler Drugstore (Fifth Avenue and 20th Street).

6 APRIL, SATURDAY

The Rev. Fred Shuttlesworth leads a march toward City Hall, beginning at the A. G. Gaston Motel; police halt the march at 18th Street and Fifth Avenue, arresting 32 participants.

7 APRIL, PALM SUNDAY

The Rev. A. D. King, the Rev. Nelson Smith, and **the Rev. John Porter** lead a march beginning at St. Paul Methodist Church (Sixth Avenue and 15th Street); police dogs are used to disperse black onlookers.

10 APRIL, WEDNESDAY

Sit-ins are attempted, but lunch counters are closed; police arrest 27 protesters in the 400 block of 19th Street.

11 APRIL, THURSDAY

Dr. Martin Luther King Jr. and other leaders receive a court-ordered injunction against "boycotting, trespassing, parading, picketing, sit-ins, kneel-ins, wade-ins, and inciting or encouraging such acts."

12 APRIL, GOOD FRIDAY

Dr. King, the Rev. Ralph Abernathy, and Shuttlesworth lead a march in defiance of the injunction and are arrested within yards of the site of the Palm Sunday arrests. During his incarceration for this offense, Dr. King writes his "Letter from Birmingham Jail."

14 APRIL, EASTER SUNDAY

Blacks attend worship services at predominantly white churches and are turned away from several other churches. Approximately 1,000 people attempt to march to City Hall but are stopped by police; 32 are arrested.

17 **APRIL, WEDNESDAY**

A local pastor and 15 black women march from the Sixteenth Street Baptist Church to the Jefferson County Courthouse to register to vote; they are arrested in the 1600 block of Sixth Avenue.

Birmingham City Council members, meeting in their second session, transfer all authority of the "former city commissioners" to themselves. The three commissioners refuse to leave, contend that they are still the official government, and ignore the council.

18 **APRIL, THURSDAY**

Demonstrators stage two sit-ins at lunch counters: one of the facilities is closed, and demonstrators are not served at the other.

19 **APRIL, FRIDAY**

Eleven protesters are arrested at the 2121 Building lunch counter.

20 **APRIL, SATURDAY**

Seven picketers outside the Pizitz lunch counter are arrested. Seven protesters are arrested at a sit-in at Britt's. Four people are arrested inside Atlantic Mills. And seven people are arrested inside at Tillman Levenson.

21 **APRIL, SUNDAY**

Fifteen black worshippers attend white church services; others are turned away.

22 **APRIL, MONDAY**

Sit-ins take place at the Woolworth's, H. L. Green, and Britt's lunch counters. Demonstrators are not served, and no arrests are made.

Presiding Judge J. Edgar Bowron hears a suit by Birmingham's new mayor and city council members seeking to oust the city commissioners.

23 **APRIL, TUESDAY**

Bowron rules in favor of Boutwell, saying the newly elected mayor and the nine recently elected council members are the legal city government.

24 **APRIL, WEDNESDAY, THROUGH MAY 1**

Sporadic demonstrations take place. Protesters spend much of their energy in the courtroom, fighting the injunction and contempt-of-court charges. Mass meetings continue at various churches.

26 **APRIL, FRIDAY**

Striking Birmingham Transit Co. bus drivers vote 201 to 162 to go back to work.

1 MAY, WEDNESDAY

Judge William Jenkins hands down sentences for five days in jail and $50 fines for 11 leaders held in contempt of court for ignoring his April 11 injunction.

2 MAY, THURSDAY

Children demonstrate en masse against the Birmingham Police Department and Commissioner Bull Connor. Nearly 1,000 children are arrested, most in groups ranging in size from 30–60.

3–4 MAY, FRIDAY AND SATURDAY

Demonstrations involving children continue. Connor responds with police dogs and water hoses, infuriating demonstrators and onlookers.

5 MAY, SUNDAY

A mass rally is held at the New Pilgrim Baptist Church (Sixth Avenue and 10th Street South). The rally culminates with a march to the Southside jail and a massive demonstration in Memorial Park across from the jail.

6 MAY, MONDAY

Several groups of children and adults that had assembled at the Sixteenth Street Baptist Church are arrested.

7 MAY, TUESDAY

Children continue to demonstrate. Shuttlesworth is hospitalized with injuries inflicted by high-powered water hoses on the steps on the Sixteenth Street Baptist Church.

8 MAY, WEDNESDAY

Demonstrations are suspended. Movement leaders say white business leaders are acting in good faith to settle issues of concern.

10 MAY, FRIDAY

Leaders of the demonstrations, represented by Dr. King, and the white business community, represented by Sidney Smyer, reach an agreement including an end to demonstrations and a cooling-off period.

From left: Dr. Martin Luther King Jr., the Rev. Fred Shuttlesworth and the Rev. Ralph Abernathy

11 MAY, SATURDAY

The **A. G. Gaston Motel** and the home of the Rev. Alfred Daniel (A.D.) King are bombed. Three people are injured in the Gaston Motel explosion. King's family escapes injury.

12 MAY, SUNDAY

President John Fitzgerald Kennedy sends U.S. troops trained in riot control to military bases near Birmingham and pledges that the federal government will "do whatever must be done" to preserve order in the strife-torn city.

20 MAY, MONDAY

The Birmingham Board of Education issues an order directing the expulsion of 1,081 black students arrested in Birmingham racial demonstrations.

22 MAY, WEDNESDAY

A federal judge rules that the children were illegally expelled and orders the student demonstrators to return to class.

23 MAY, THURSDAY

Alabama Supreme Court backs Birmingham voters in their decision to change to a mayor-council form of government.

More than 1,000 black student demonstrators return to class under a federal judge's order that they had been illegally expelled.

28 MAY, TUESDAY

U.S. District Judge Seybourn H. Lynne refuses to order desegregation of Birmingham schools.

Students were taught that civil disobedience was a key part of the Movement's nonviolent strategy.

11 JUNE, TUESDAY

Federal troops head to the University of Alabama to enforce enrollment of two blacks as **Gov. Wallace** "stands in the schoolhouse door."

19 JUNE, WEDNESDAY

Local police and helmeted state troopers, using nightsticks and electric cattle prods, move in Gadsden and disperse more than 300 black protestors from the courthouse lawn.

The Birmingham Parks and Recreation Board votes to reopen at least three municipal golf courses by June 29.

2 JULY, TUESDAY

Plans to merge the Bank for Savings and Trust into the Birmingham Trust National Bank are approved by directors of both banks.

10 JULY, WEDNESDAY

Alabama's Highway Director serves notice that the state is ready to proceed with construction of the second section of the six-lane, $16 million Red Mountain Expressway.

12 JULY, FRIDAY

The Fifth U.S. Circuit Court of Appeals orders Birmingham to begin desegregating public schools by fall.

16 JULY, TUESDAY

About 200 Birmingham citizens answer a challenge from Mayor Boutwell to serve as members of the new Community Affairs Committee.

A school meeting on desegregation of public schools ends in disorder after some speakers are drowned out.

3 AUGUST, SATURDAY

About 300 are jailed in Gadsden after law-enforcement officers break up a mass anti-segregation demonstration in downtown streets.

7 AUGUST, WEDNESDAY

The Birmingham City Council adopts Mayor Boutwell's $15 million general fund budget for fiscal year 1963–1964.

15 AUGUST, THURSDAY

A man sets off a tear-gas bomb on the main floor of **Loveman's** department store, sending at least 22 people to local hospitals.

19 AUGUST, MONDAY

Judge Clarence Allgood approves the Birmingham Board of Education's desegregation plan, as demanded in by the Fifth Circuit Court of Appeals; the plan is for Birmingham city schools to begin integrating 12th grade classes.

29 **JUNE, SATURDAY**
Birmingham Police Chief Jamie Moore asks for a $540,000 increase in the police budget for the 1963–1964 fiscal year, emphasizing the heavy load placed on **policemen** during race-related demonstrations.

19 **JULY, FRIDAY**
Boutwell presents City Council a $15,050,270 budget for the 1963–1964 fiscal year.

23 **JULY, TUESDAY**
The Birmingham City Council unanimously repeals all segregation ordinances as provided in the city's General Code.

24 **JULY, WEDNESDAY**
Fourteen hours after a powerful lightning storm rips through the Birmingham area, nine neighborhoods are still without power.

28 **JULY, SUNDAY**
The City Federal Savings and Loan Association moves into its modernized new home in the former Comer Building in downtown Birmingham.

31 **JULY, WEDNESDAY**
The U.S. Justice Department files suit against the Jefferson County Board of Registrars requiring the board to instate more than 2,000 black voter applicants who were rejected because they failed county qualification tests.

20 **AUGUST, TUESDAY**
A bomb explodes and damages home of attorney Arthur D. Shores; there are no injuries.

21 **AUGUST, WEDNESDAY**
Black attorneys ask for a federal court order requiring the Board of Education to begin desegregation on all grade levels in the fall instead of only the 12th grade as planned.

27 **AUGUST, TUESDAY**
Six buses leave the Sixteenth Street Baptist Church headed for Washington, D.C., to participate in the March on Washington for Jobs and Freedom.

28 **AUGUST, WEDNESDAY**
Dr. King refers to the violence in Alabama in his historic "I Have a Dream" speech, delivered on the steps of the Lincoln Memorial

30 **AUGUST, FRIDAY**
Birmingham School Board attorneys announce that the three schools to be desegregated are West End and Ramsay high schools and Graymont Elementary School; five blacks are to be enrolled at the schools.

3 SEPTEMBER, TUESDAY

The Birmingham City Council votes to approve the sale of Birmingham Transit Co., to American Transit Co. of St. Louis.

4 SEPTEMBER, WEDNESDAY

Police battle demonstrators at Graymont Elementary School and Ramsay High School, with many **protesters** waving Confederate flags and anti-desegregation placards.

For the second time in 15 days, a bomb damages the home attorney Shores; his wife suffers a minor shoulder injury.

5 SEPTEMBER, THURSDAY

The Birmingham Board of Education formally closes three public schools.

8 SEPTEMBER, SUNDAY

Bombers hurl two firebombs at the suburban home of businessman Arthur George (A.G) Gaston.

6 OCTOBER, SUNDAY

Eighty-eight mostly white civic leaders and residents publish a full-page ad in *The Birmingham News* asking the mayor and city council to consider the hiring of black policemen.

20 OCTOBER, SUNDAY

More than 500,000 Jefferson County citizens participate in the first of the Sabin Oral Sundays to strike a blow against paralytic polio.

One-hundred-sixteen black residents publish a **full-page ad** in *The Birmingham News*, titled "Birmingham's Moment of Crisis: A Statement of Concern and Conviction," asking for the city to take action in several areas to address the tense racial climate.

22 OCTOBER, TUESDAY

City officials reject proposals for hiring black policemen.

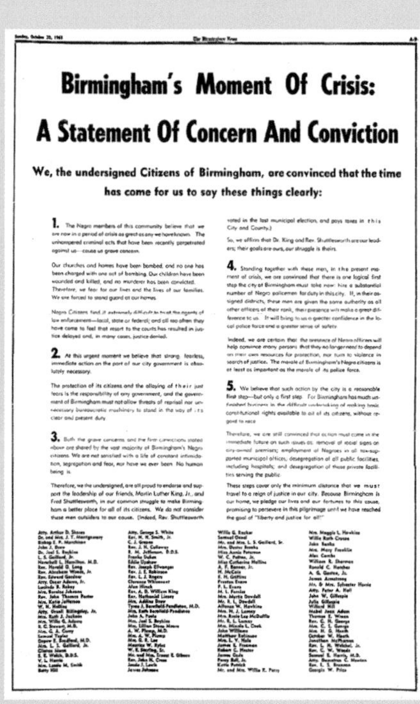

Birmingham's Moment Of Crisis:

A Statement Of Concern And Conviction

We, the undersigned Citizens of Birmingham, are convinced that the time has come for us to say these things clearly:

1. The Negro members of this community believe that we are now in a period of crisis as great as any we have known. The unhampered criminal acts that have been recently perpetrated against us—cause us grave concern.

Our churches and homes have been bombed, and no one has been charged with one act of bombing. Our children have been wounded and killed, and no murderer has been convicted. Therefore, we fear for our lives and the lives of our families. We are forced to stand guard at our homes.

Negro Citizens find it extremely difficult to trust the agents of law enforcement—local, state or federal; and all too often they have come to feel that resort to the courts has resulted in justice delayed and, in many cases, justice denied.

2. At this urgent moment we believe that strong, fearless, immediate action on the part of our city government is absolutely necessary.

The protection of its citizens and the allaying of their just fears is the responsibility of any government, and the government of Birmingham must not allow threats of reprisal nor unnecessary bureaucratic machinery to stand in the way of its clear and present duty.

3. Both the grave concerns and the firm convictions stated above are shared by the vast majority of Birmingham's Negro citizens. We are not satisfied with a life of constant intimidation, segregation and fear, nor have we ever been. No human being is.

Therefore, we the undersigned, are all proud to endorse and support the leadership of our friends, Martin Luther King, Jr., and Fred Shuttlesworth, in our common struggle to make Birmingham a better place for all of its citizens. We do not consider these men outsiders to our cause. (Indeed, Rev. Shuttlesworth voted in the last municipal election, and pays taxes in this City and County.)

So, we affirm that Dr. King and Rev. Shuttlesworth are our leaders; their goals are ours, our struggle is theirs.

4. Standing together with these men, in the present moment of crisis, we are convinced that there is one logical first step the city of Birmingham must take now: hire a substantial number of Negro policemen for duty in this city. If, in their assigned districts, these men are given the same authority as all other officers of their rank, their presence will make a great difference to us. It will bring to us a greater confidence in the local police force and a greater sense of safety.

Indeed, we are certain that the presence of Negro officers will help convince many persons that they no longer need to depend on their own resources for protection, nor turn to violence in search of justice. The morale of Birmingham's Negro citizens is at least as important as the morale of its police force.

5. We believe that such action by the city is a reasonable first step—but only a first step. For Birmingham has much unfinished business in the difficult undertaking of making basic constitutional rights available to all of its citizens, without regard to race.

Therefore, we are still convinced that action must come in the immediate future on such issues as: removal of racial signs on city-owned premises; employment of Negroes in all tax-supported municipal offices; desegregation of all public facilities, including hospitals; and desegregation of those private facilities serving the public.

These steps cover only the minimum distance that we must travel to a reign of justice in our city. Because Birmingham is our home, we pledge our lives and our fortunes to this cause, promising to persevere in this pilgrimage until we have reached the goal of "liberty and justice for all!"

9 SEPTEMBER, MONDAY
Gov. Wallace bars blacks from five state schools, which had been ordered by the schools to accept them. Alabama state troopers turn back blacks in Birmingham, Tuskegee, and Mobile.

10 SEPTEMBER, TUESDAY
President Kennedy orders the **Alabama National Guard** federalized and tells Secretary of Defense Robert McNamara to use any of the nation's armed forces he deemsa necessary to enforce school desegregation in Alabama.

15 SEPTEMBER, SUNDAY
The **Sixteenth Street Baptist Church** is bombed; four girls are killed—14-year-olds Cynthia Wesley, Carole Robertson, and Addie Mae Collins, and 11-year-old Denise McNair.

17 SEPTEMBER, TUESDAY
Funeral service for Robertson is held at St. John's A.M.E. Church.

18 SEPTEMBER, WEDNESDAY
Funeral service for Wesley, Collins, and McNair is held at Sixth Avenue Baptist Church.

22 NOVEMBER, FRIDAY
President Kennedy is assassinated in Dallas.

25 NOVEMBER, MONDAY
Birmingham city offices and churches join in a final formal tribute to President Kennedy.

13 DECEMBER, FRIDAY
State officials announce an agreement to begin immediate construction of the Red Mountain Expressway bridge over 21st Street.

23 DECEMBER, MONDAY
Six black children, ranging in age from seven months to six years, die in a fire that raged through their home in Collegeville.

25 DECEMBER, WEDNESDAY
A 14-year-old Woodlawn High School student missing for two days is found frozen to death in an open ditch near Eastwood Mall. The death was from a fall and exposure to the elements, although an autopsy was ordered.

Sources: *Birmingham Post-Herald*; *The Birmingham News*; Huntley, Horace and John W. McKerley, *Foot Soldiers for Democracy: The Men, Women, and Children of the Birmingham Civil Rights Movement*. Champaign: University of Illinois Press, 2009.

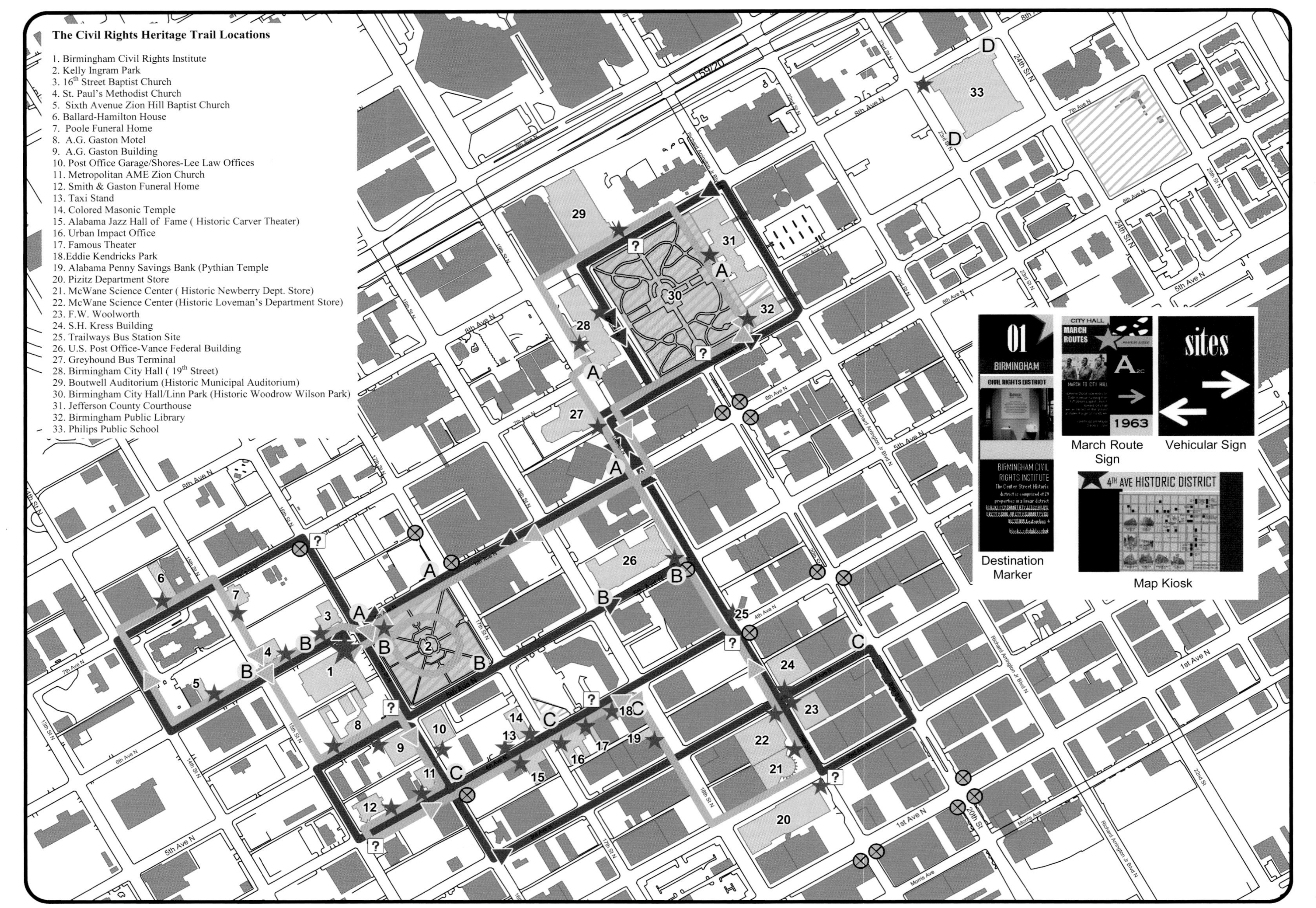

The Civil Rights Heritage Trail Locations
1. Birmingham Civil Rights Institute
2. Kelly Ingram Park
3. 16th Street Baptist Church
4. St. Paul's Methodist Church
5. Sixth Avenue Zion Hill Baptist Church
6. Ballard-Hamilton House
7. Poole Funeral Home
8. A.G. Gaston Motel
9. A.G. Gaston Building
10. Post Office Garage/Shores-Lee Law Offices
11. Metropolitan AME Zion Church
12. Smith & Gaston Funeral Home
13. Taxi Stand
14. Colored Masonic Temple
15. Alabama Jazz Hall of Fame (Historic Carver Theater)
16. Urban Impact Office
17. Famous Theater
18.Eddie Kendricks Park
19. Alabama Penny Savings Bank (Pythian Temple
20. Pizitz Department Store
21. McWane Science Center (Historic Newberry Dept. Store)
22. McWane Science Center (Historic Loveman's Department Store)
23. F.W. Woolworth
24. S.H. Kress Building
25. Trailways Bus Station Site
26. U.S. Post Office-Vance Federal Building
27. Greyhound Bus Terminal
28. Birmingham City Hall (19th Street)
29. Boutwell Auditorium (Historic Municipal Auditorium)
30. Birmingham City Hall/Linn Park (Historic Woodrow Wilson Park)
31. Jefferson County Courthouse
32. Birmingham Public Library
33. Philips Public School
Destination Marker
March Route Sign
Vehicular Sign
Map Kiosk
01
BIRMINGHAM
CIVIL RIGHTS DISTRICT
BIRMINGHAM CIVIL RIGHTS INSTITUTE
CITY HALL
MARCH ROUTES
MARCH TO CITY HALL
1963
sites
4TH AVE HISTORIC DISTRICT
I-59/20
8th Ave N
7th Ave N
6th Ave N
5th Ave N
4th Ave N
1st Ave N
Richard Arrington Jr Blvd N
Morris Ave
13th St N
14th St N
15th St N
16th St N
17th St N
18th St N
20th St
22nd St
23rd St N
24th St N
25th St N

Birmingham Civil Rights Heritage Trail

The Civil Rights Heritage Trail Project

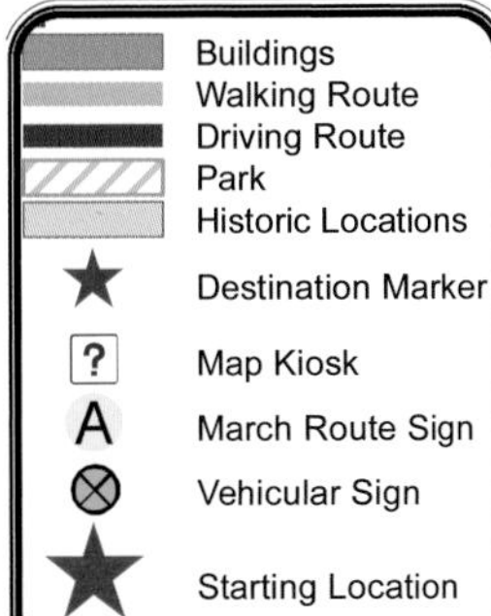

Map Prepared by City of Birmingham GIS Division

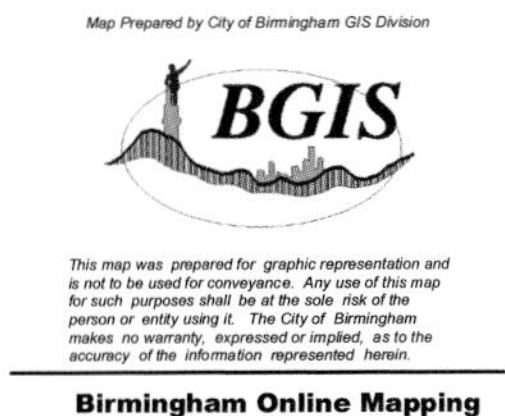

This map was prepared for graphic representation and is not to be used for conveyance. Any use of this map for such purposes shall be at the sole risk of the person or entity using it. The City of Birmingham makes no warranty, expressed or implied, as to the accuracy of the information represented herein.

Birmingham Online Mapping
Internet (Public Access)
http://gisweb.informationbirmingham.com
Intranet (City Employees)
http://gisweb

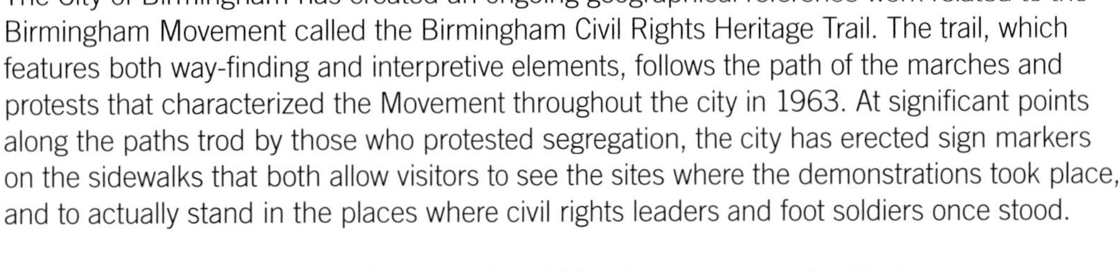

The City of Birmingham has created an ongoing geographical reference work related to the Birmingham Movement called the Birmingham Civil Rights Heritage Trail. The trail, which features both way-finding and interpretive elements, follows the path of the marches and protests that characterized the Movement throughout the city in 1963. At significant points along the paths trod by those who protested segregation, the city has erected sign markers on the sidewalks that both allow visitors to see the sites where the demonstrations took place, and to actually stand in the places where civil rights leaders and foot soldiers once stood.

Research, interviews and text for more than 200 trail signs was crafted by former *Birmingham News* Reporter, Vickii Howell, now CEO of Avant Media.

Renee Kemp-Rotan, Director of Grants and Special Projects and Director of the Birmingham Civil Rights Heritage Trail, designed the original prototypes for these highly interactive signs. Each of the colorful steel markers is 80 inches tall and features a cutout of a walking or marching person. "Some thought the 80-inch tall signs to be too big," wrote Kemp-Rotan. "However, this size made it plain and simple; these signs are too big for history here in Birmingham to ever be denied." Soon multi-media access to the signs will be available through QR codes and smart phones with original voice-overs from actual Birmingham Foot Soldiers.

Through the cutouts a visitor can see important places targeted for non-violent mass action by Fred L. Shuttlesworth, Dr. Martin Luther King Jr., and those who followed in the struggle to end segregated services, business practices, and schooling, and to bring an end to terrorist acts by the Ku Klux Klan and others perpetrated against black citizens and others in their homes, businesses, and churches. The markers also include historic photographs (some reproduced in this book) provided by *The Birmingham News*, the Birmingham Public Library, the Birmingham Civil Rights Institute, the Associated Press, and Corbis Images, as well as curated headlines and text explaining the significance of the particular area where a given sign stands.

The markers are located primarily in downtown Birmingham's Civil Rights District, at sites near City Hall, the Jefferson County Courthouse, Linn Park, Kelly Ingram Park, and Sixteenth Street Baptist Church, for example. Other sites where markers are or are scheduled to be erected include the Bethel Baptist Church District, Center Street /Dynamite Hill, The Birmingham Jail District and the Birmingham Shuttlesworth International Airport as part of a Gateway to Civil Rights theme connected to the major airport renovation project.

The original 1963 march routes are listed on the National Register of Historic Places, thanks to the work of Marjorie White, executive director of the Birmingham Historical Society. The heritage trail signage routes are organized as The March to Government, The March to Retail, The March For Education, F.L.Shuttlesworth and the Purposeful Life.

You can see the layout of the Birmingham Civil Rights Heritage Trail on the facing page. For more information about the trail, its history and further development, visit www.informationbirmingham.com.

Notes

[1] Carolyn Maull McKinstry, *Foot Soldiers for Democracy: The Men, Women, and Children of The Birmingham Civil Rights Movement*, University of Illinois Press, 2009. Edited by Horace Huntley and John W. McKerley, page 157.

[2] Ibid.

[3] Diane McWhorter, *Carry Me Home, Birmingham, Alabama: The Climatic Battle of the Civil Rights Revolution.* A Touchstone Book Published by Simon and Schuster, 2002. Page 23.

[4] *Birmingham Post-Herald*, Dec. 24, 1963.

[5] Dr. Martin Luther King Jr. "Letter from Birmingham Jail"

[6] Odessa Woolfolk, educator and civil rights activist, in *Black Workers' Struggle for Equality in Birmingham.* University of Illinois Press. 2007. Edited by Horace Huntley and David Montgomery. Page 228.

[7] Huntley and Montgomery, *Black Workers' Struggle for Equality in Birmingham.* Page vii.

[8] Woolfolk *Black Workers' Struggle for Equality in Birmingham*, page 228; John Hope Franklin, *From Slavery to Freedom: A History of African Americans*, 3rd Edition. (New York: Alfred A. Knopf.)

History

[1] Edward Shannon LaMonte, Politics *and Welfare in Birmingham, 1900-1975.* (The University of Alabama Press. 1995). Page 3; John R. Hornady, *The Book of Birmingham.* (New York: Dodd, Mead, 1921). Page 169

[2] LaMonte, *Politics and Welfare in Birmingham*, Page 3; Martha Carolyn Mitchell Bigelow "Birmingham: Biography of a City of the New South" (Ph.D dissertation, University of Chicago, 1946). Page 13.

[3] Hornady, *The Book of Birmingham*, Page 20.

[4] Bigelow, Page 21.

[5] LaMonte, Pages 5–6; George B. Ward: *Birmingham's Urban Statesman*, (Birmingham: Birmingham Public Library, 1974). Page 31.

[6] LaMonte, Page 10; Bigelow, Page 220.

[7] LaMonte. Page 10; *The Birmingham News*, Nov. 22, 1905.

[8] LaMonte, Page 11; *The Birmingham News*, Nov. 5, 1903.

[9] LaMonte, Page 11; *The Birmingham News*, March 7, 1905.

[10] LaMonte, Page 14. Bigelow, Page 79.

[11] LaMonte,. Page 14; Malcolm Cook McMillan, Constitutional Development in Alabama, 1798-1901: A Study in Politics, The Negro, and Sectionalism (Chapel Hill: University of North Carolina Press, 1955 (Vol. 37 of James Sprunt Studies in History and Political Science); Spartansburg, S.C.: Reprint Company, 1978) pp. v, 370.

[12] LaMonte, Page 14; *The Birmingham News*, Feb. 19, 1902.

[13] LaMonte,_ Page 74.

[14] Ibid.

[15] Ibid.

[16] LaMonte, Page 73.

[17] *The Birmingham News*, Aug. 21, 1963.

[18] Ibid.

[19] LaMonte, Page 137

[20] LaMonte, Page 137; Richard Kluger, *Simple Justice: The History of Brown v. Board of Education*

and Black America's Struggle for Equality (New York: Vintage Books, 1977). Page 752.

[21] Birmingham Historical Society, Page 2.

[22] Ibid. Page iv.

[23] Ibid.

[24] LaMonte, Page 164; Robert Gaines Corley, The Quest for Racial Harmony: Race Relations in Birmingham, Alabama, 1947-1963 (Ph.D. dissertation, University of Virginia, 1979). Page 217.

[25] LaMonte, Page 164.

[26] Ibid.

[27] Ibid.

[28] *The Birmingham News*, July 13, 1997

[29] Ibid.

January to March

[1] *The Birmingham News*, Jan. 1, 1963

[2] *The Birmingham News*, Jan. 12, 1963

[3] Ibid.

[4] *The Birmingham News*, Jan. 14, 1963

[5] Ibid.

[6] Taylor Branch, *Parting the Waters: America in the Kings Years, 1953-1963*. New York: Simon & Schuster, 1988. Page 688.

[7] Branch, Page 689.

[8] *Birmingham Post-Herald*, Feb.15, 1963.

[9] *The Birmingham News*, Feb. 20, 1963.

[10] LaMonte. Page 73.

[11] *Birmingham Post-Herald*, March 6, 1973.

[12] Ibid.

[13] *Birmingham Post-Herald*, March 25, 1963.

[14] *Birmingham Post-Herald*, April 2, 1963.

April

[1] *Birmingham Post-Herald*, April 3, 1963.

[2] *The Birmingham News*, April 3, 1963.

[3] Ibid.

[4] *Birmingham Post-Herald*, April 3, 1963.

[5] Ibid.

[6] LaMonte. Page 175; *Birmingham Post-Herald*, April 15, 17, 29, 1963.

[7] LaMonte, Page 175.

[8] Ibid.

[9] LaMonte, Page 176.

[10] Huntley and McKerley, *Foot Soldiers for Democracy*, Page xvi.

[11] Ibid.

[12] Ibid.

[13] Elizabeth Fitts in Huntley and McKerley, *Foot Soldiers for Democracy*, Page 106.

[14] Branch, Page 727.

[15] Huntley and McKerley, page xxvii.

[16] Jonathan McPherson in Huntley and McKerley, *Foot Soldiers for Democracy*, Page 86.

[17] Ibid.

[18] Carlton Reese in Huntley and McKerley, *Foot Soldiers for Democracy*, Page 102; Reese died on July 9, 2002.

[19] Ibid.

[20] Huntley and McKerley, page xxviii.

[21] Joe N. Dickson in Huntley and McKerley, *Foot Soldiers for Democracy*, Page 74.

[22] Ibid.

[23] Johnnie McKinstry Summerville in Huntley and McKerley, *Foot Soldiers for Democracy*. Page 80.

[24] Ibid.

[25] Huntley and McKerley, pages xxviii–xxix.

[26] Annetta Streeter Gary in Huntley and McKerley, *Foot Soldiers for Democracy*, Page 118.

[27] Ibid.

[28] Huntley and McKerley, page xxix.

[29] Ibid.

[30] *Birmingham Post-Herald*, April 18, 1963

[31] *Birmingham Post-Herald*, April 24, 1963

[32] *Birmingham Post-Herald*, April 27, 1963

May

[1] McWhorter, Pages 366–368.

[2] Huntley and McKerley, Page xxix.

[3] Branch, Pages 756–757.

[4] McWhorter, Pages 366–372.

[5] *The Birmingham News*, May 4, 1963.

[6] Carolyn Maull McKinstry in Huntley and McKerley, *Foot Soldiers for Democracy*, Page 155.

[7] Annetta Streeter Gary in Huntley and McKerley, *Foot Soldiers for Democracy.* Page 120.

[8] Ibid.

[9] McWhorter, Page 369.

[10] McWhorter, Pages 366–372.

[11] Branch, Pages 760.

[12] Huntley and McKerley, Page xxix.

[13] Huntley and McKerley, Page xxx.

[14] Annetta Streeter Gary in Huntley and McKerley, *Foot Soldiers for Democracy,* Page 120.

[15] Willie Casey in Huntley and McKerley, *Foot Soldiers for Democracy,* Page 128.

[16] Ibid.

[17] Nims R. Gay in Huntley and McKerley, *Foot Soldiers for Democracy,* Page 34.

[18] Ibid.

[19] Huntley and Montgomery, *Black Workers' Struggle for Equality in Birmingham*, Page 168.

[20] Ibid.

[21] Huntley and McKerley, Page 30.

[22] Branch, Page 770.

[23] Ibid.

[24] Ibid.

[25] Branch, Page 775.

[26] Ibid.

[27] McWhorter, page 405.

[28] Ibid.

[29] Emma Smith Young in Huntley and McKerley, *Foot Soldiers for Democracy,* Page 4; Young died in 2004 at the age of 102.

[30] Ibid.

[31] Malcolm Hooks in Huntley and McKerley, *Foot Soldiers for Democracy,* Page 170.

[32] Ibid.

[33] Joe N. Dickson in Huntley and McKerley, *Foot Soldiers for Democracy.* Page 74.

[34] Ibid.

[35] LaMonte, Page 182.

[36] *The Birmingham News,* May 11, 1963.

[37] McWhorter, Page 422.

[38] Ibid.

[39] Ibid.

[40] *The Birmingham News,* May 11, 1963.

[41] *The Birmingham News,* May 12, 1963.

[42] Ibid.

[43] Ibid.

[44] *Birmingham Post-Herald,* May 13 1963.

[45] *Birmingham News,* May 13, 1963.

[46] *Birmingham Post-Herald,* May 23, 1963.

[47] Ibid.

[48] *The Birmingham News,* May 28, 1963.

June to August

[1] Branch, pages 806, 825.

[2] *The Birmingham News,* Aug. 3, 1963.

[3] The *Birmingham News,* June 11, 1963; *Birmingham Post-Herald,* June 12, 1963

[4] *The Birmingham News,* June 11, 1963

[5] Ibid.

[6] *Birmingham Post-Herald,* June 12, 1963

[7] *The Birmingham News* and *Birmingham Post-Herald,* June 1963–August 1963

[8] Lee, Helen Shores and Barbara S. Shores, *The Gentle Giant of Dynamite Hill: The Untold Story of Arthur Shores and His Family's Fight for Civil Rights.* Zondervan, 2012. Pages 33-34.

[9] *The Birmingham News* and *Birmingham Post-Herald,* June 1963–August 1963

September

[1] *The Birmingham News*, Sept. 4, 1963
[2] Ibid.
[3] Ibid.
[4] Ibid.
[5] Ibid.
[6] Ibid.
[7] *The Birmingham News*, Sept. 5, 1963
[8] Ibid.
[9] *The Birmingham News*, Sept. 8, 1963
[10] A 1965 FBI memo to agency director J. Edgar Hoover named Robert E. Chambliss, Bobby Frank Cherry, Herman Frank Cash, and Thomas E. Blanton, all locals and alleged Klansmen, as possible culprits. The FBI closed its investigation in 1968, however, without filing any charges. A 1980 U.S. Justice Department investigation concluded that Hoover had prevented agents from disclosing their findings to prosecutors.
Three former Klansmen were later convicted of the Sixteenth Street Baptist Church bombing. Robert Chambliss was convicted in 1977; he died in prison in 1985. Bobby Frank Cherry was convicted in 2002; he died in 2004. Thomas Blanton Jr. was convicted in 2001; now 82 years old, he remains imprisoned at the St. Clair Correctional Facility in St. Clair County, Ala. Cash, who was never charged in the case, died in 1994.
[11] *The Birmingham News*, Sept. 15, 1963
[12] The Rev. John Cross, The Birmingham Civil Rights Institute: Oral History Project
[13] Ibid.
[14] Ibid.
[15] *Birmingham Post-Herald*, Sept. 15, 1988.
[16] Ibid.
[17] *Birmingham Post-Herald*, Dec. 24, 1963.
[18] Carolyn Maull McKinstry in Huntley and McKerley, *Foot Soldiers for Democracy*, Pages 156–160.
[19] Ibid.
[20] Annetta Streeter Gary in Huntley and McKerley, *Foot Soldiers for Democracy*, Page 118.
[21] Ibid
[22] James Ware and Melvin Ware in Huntley and McKerley, *Foot Soldiers for Democracy*, Pages 122–125.
[23] Huntley and McKerley, Page 126.
[24] Ibid.
[25] *The Birmingham News*, Sept. 15, 1988.
[26] *The Birmingham News*, Sept. 16, 1963.
[27] *The Birmingham News*, Sept. 18, 1963.
[28] *The Birmingham News*, Sept. 19, 1963.
[29] Ibid.
[30] Ibid.

October to December

[1] Leroy Stover became Birmingham's first black police officer on March 30, 1966.
[2] *The Birmingham News*, Oct. 22, 1963.
[3] Ibid.
[4] *The Birmingham News*, Nov. 25, 1963
[5] *Birmingham World*, Nov. 27, 1963
[6] Ibid.
[7] Ibid.
[8] Ibid.
[9] *The Birmingham News*, Nov. 25, 1963
[10] Ibid.
[11] *Birmingham Post-Herald*, Dec. 13, 1963
[12] *Birmingham Post-Herald*, Dec. 24, 1963
[13] Ibid.
[14] *Birmingham Post-Herald*, Dec. 26, 1963.
[15] *The Birmingham News*, Jan. 1, 1964.

Epilogue

[1] *The Birmingham News*, Jan. 1, 1964.

Bibliography

1. Abernathy, Ralph David. *And the Walls Came Tumbling Down.* New York, N.Y.: Harper Collins. 1991

2. The Birmingham Civil Rights Institute: Oral History Project. July 24, 1997.

3. The Birmingham Historical Society. *A Walk to Freedom: The Rev. Fred Shuttlesworth and the Alabama Christian Movement for Human Rights, 1956–1964.* Birmingham: Birmingham Historical Society.

4. *Birmingham Post-Herald*

5. *The Birmingham News*

6. *Birmingham World*

7. Bigelow Mitchell, Martha Carolyn. "Birmingham: Biography of a City in the New South." Ph.D. dissertation, University of Chicago. 1946.

8. Branch, Taylor. *Parting the Waters: America in the King Years, 1954–1963.* New York, N.Y.: Simon & Schuster, 1988.

9. Corley, Robert Gaines. "The Quest for Racial Harmony: Race Relations in Birningham, Alabama, 1947-1963." Ph.D. dissertation, University of Virginia. 1979.

10. Cross, John. "Birmingham Civil Rights Institute: Oral History Project." 1997.

11. Eskew, Glenn T. *But for Birmingham: The Local and National Movement in the Civil Rights Struggle.* The University of North Carolina Press. Chapel Hill and London. 1997.

12. Franklin, John Hope. *From Slavery to Freedom: A History of Negro Americans. 3rd. Edition.* New York, N.Y.: Vintage Books, Alfred A. Knopf, 1969.

13. Gross, Terry. NPR. January 12, 2006. Accessed July 27, 2012 <http://www.npr.org/templates/story/story.php?storyId=5149667>.

14. Hrabowski, Freeman. Interview. September, 2012.

15. Hornady, John R. *The Book of Birmingham.* New York, N.Y.: Dodd, Mead, and Co., 1921.

16. Huntley, Horace and David Montgomery, *Black Workers' Struggle for Equality in Birmingham.* Champaign, Ill.: University of Illinois Press, 2007.

17. Huntley, Horace and John W. McKerley, *Foot Soldiers for Democracy: The Men, Women, and Children of the Birmingham Civil Rights Movement.* Champaign, Ill.: University of Illinois Press, 2009.

18. King, Martin Luther Jr. "Letter from Birmingham Jail." Birmingham, Ala., April 16, 1963.

19. Kluger, Richard. *Simple Justice: The History of Brown v. Board of Education and Black America's Struggle for Equality.* New York, N.Y.: Vintage Books, 1977.

20. LaMonte, Edward Shannon. *George B. Ward: Birmingham's Urban Statesman.* Birmingham, Ala.: Birmingham Public Library, 1974.

21. LaMonte. *Politics and Welfare in Birmingham, 1900–1975.* Tuscaloosa, Ala.: University of Alabama Press, 1995.

22. LaMonte. Interview with Barnett Wright, September, 10, 2012.

23. Lee, Helen Shores and Barbara S. Shores, *The Gentle Giant of Dynamite Hill: The Untold Story of Arthur Shores and His Family's Fight for Civil Rights.* Zondervan, 2012.

24. Lee. Helen Shores. Interview with Barnett Wright. September, 12, 2012.

25. McMillan, Malcolm Cook. *The James Sprunt Studies in History and Political Science—Constitutional Development in Alabama 1798–1901: A Study in Politics, the Negro, and Sectionalism.* Vol. 37. Chapel Hill, N.C.: University of North Carolina Press, 1955.

26. McWhorter, Diane. *Carry Me Home, Birmingham, Alabama: The Climactic Battle of the Civil Rights Revolution.* New York, N.Y: A Touchstone Book, Simon & Schuster, 2002.

27. Rotch, Jim. Interview with Barnett Wright. September, 12, 2012.

28. Roberts, Gene and Klibanoff, Hank. *The Race Beat: The Press, the Civil Rights Struggle and the Awakening of a Nation.* Knopf, 1st Edition. 2006.

29. Williams, Anderson. Interview with Barnett Wright. July, 10, 2012.

Voices from the Movement

"When visitors are brought to Birmingham, the Civil Rights Institute is very typically included on the short list of must see places. That means 'must see' the ugly history, the pain of what the community went through and the gradual but consistent evolution in maturing that has taken place."

Edward Shannon LaMonte, a retired professor of political science from Birmingham Southern College

"In the name of the greatest people that have ever trod this earth, I draw the line in the dust and toss the gauntlet before the feet of tyranny ... and I say ... segregation now ... segregation tomorrow ... segregation forever!"

Governor George C. Wallace during his inauguration

"I see it as hope for every family whose breadwinner is out of a job. I look on it as an open invitation from the citizens of Birmingham to all our neighbors to merge their interests and boundaries with ours."

Albert Boutwell, after being elected Birmingham mayor

"In Birmingham during Easter week in 1963, I was arrested for demonstrating and placed in jail with older women who participated in the movement. There were no mattresses on our cots, so we used our coats to make pads for the older women to sleep on. ... I spent four days in that jail, and the food was horrible. The grits were brown, the eggs were powdered, and the biscuits were hard."

Elizabeth Fitts, of Titusville, who took part in the anti-segregation campaigns of 1962 and 1963

"Shallow understanding from people of good will is more frustrating than absolute misunderstanding from people of ill will. Lukewarm acceptance is more bewildering that outright rejection."

Dr. Martin Luther King Jr. "Letter From Birmingham Jail"

"Many of us got beat on, but we kept going. We were instructed to keep going and not fight back because fighting back would only make the police retaliate."

Carlton Reese, an organist at New Pilgrim Baptist Church

"We were really putting ourselves on the line and we never thought about it. We never thought about being killed, being hurt, or being fired. We knew that it was necessary."

Johnnie McKinstry Summerville, a teacher and a regular at mass meetings during the Birmingham Movement

"I was arrested on Saturday morning, and I stayed until Monday night. It was an experience that just can't be explained. I remember the closing of the doors ..."

Annetta Streeter Gary, member of the Peace Ponies, an all-girls club that supported the movement

"The water hoses hurt a lot. I was hit with the water hose ... running from water. I had a navy blue sweater on. The water tore a big hole in my sweater and swiped part of my hair off on that side. I just remember the sting and the pain on my face."

Carolyn Maull McKinstry, 15-year-old Parker High School student

"We started walking for about two or three blocks singing 'We Shall Overcome.' Then the cops stopped us, let the dogs out, and put us in a paddy wagon. I was in the center of the paddy wagon. They crammed us in there like sardines. It must have been thirty of us in there."

Willie Casey, Carver High School student among dozens arrested on their way to a mass meeting

"I witnessed my oldest son being washed down the street with a hose ... I would not have thought twice about hitting one of those firemen or policemen ... but there is a hereafter, and you must stand before God to be judged."

Nims R. Gay remembers one of his children being slammed by water from the hoses

"Birmingham reached an accord with its conscience today. The acceptance of responsibility by local white and Negro leadership offers an example of a free people uniting to meet and solve their problems. Birmingham may well offer for 20th-century America an example of progressive race relations, and for all mankind a dawn of a new day, a promise for all men, a day of opportunity and a new sense of freedom for America."

The Rev. Fred L. Shuttlesworth

The nation faces "a moral issue ... as old as the Scriptures and ... as clear as the American Constitution."

President John F. Kennedy on discrimination against black Americans

"The crumpled roof of our home had collapsed and hung near the ground. The garage doors had blown wide open ... the rioting terrified me. Police struggled to get control of the mayhem. Broken bottles and glass covered the street and sidewalk. Men threw bricks at police cars, lashing out in uncontrolled anger."

Barbara Sylvia Shores, daughter of attorney Arthur Shores, after a bomb ripped through their home

"It was a wonderful lesson too, 'a love that forgives'. People seem to have love, but they don't know how to forgive."

The Rev. John Cross, pastor of Sixteenth Street Baptist Church, on the lesson being taught when the church was bombed